"Mike and I share the love of Edmonton and his book *Lunch with Leaders* does an amazing job of showcasing the entrepreneurial spirit that drives our great city, along with other great cities that are referenced in this book. From humble beginnings to remarkable success, each leader's journey offers readers a glimpse into the triumphs, challenges, and lessons that shaped their careers. *Lunch with Leaders* is a must-read for anyone seeking motivation, guidance, and a deeper understanding of what it takes to thrive in the business world."

—**Dave Hardy**, CEO, Orangetheory Fitness Canada

"*Lunch with Leaders* offers an incredibly insightful look at the defining stories of successful entrepreneurs and executives. Through one-on-one interviews, Mike Mack draws out the pivotal moments and lessons that shaped each leader's journey. From overcoming adversity to solving problems creatively, their candid reflections reveal a wealth of diverse perspectives. This book is a must-read for anyone looking to gain insight into the minds of dynamic business leaders."

—**Melonie Dodaro, A**uthor of *LinkedIn Unlocked*
and *Navigating LinkedIn for Sales*

"While I have enjoyed lunch with Mike on several occasions over the years, I appreciate the concept and approach to publishing his latest book, *Lunch with Leaders*. As a leader and entrepreneur, I have a firsthand understanding of the challenges and pivotal moments that define success or failure in business. It allows all of us to reflect on the things that we did well, or perhaps consider what we would have done differently. Either way, it is the responsibility that we take on as business leaders. I encourage all entrepreneurs and leaders to take the time to read the stories within this content rich book."

—**Eddy Stahl**, Chief Executive Officer, Stahl Peterbilt Inc.

"Mike Mack understands relationships. He cultivates relationships thoughtfully, deliberately and relentlessly. In this book, he's leveraged 12 relationships to tell 12 stories that reveal the core of what motivates leaders and entrepreneurs. What richness of insight, what humour, what depth of thought, what inspiration are revealed in his conversations with these 12 leaders. How lucky we are to receive the benefit of their wisdom. There is much in this book to savour. If you are an entrepreneur, if you are a family member of an entrepreneur, or if you work with entrepreneurs, this book should be on your "must read" list."

—**Leah Tolton**, FEA, Partner, Bennett Jones LLP

"This book is a treasure trove of insights, anecdotes, and thought-provoking conversations with leaders from different walks of life. Whether you're a budding entrepreneur, a seasoned executive, or simply someone looking for inspiration, *Lunch with Leaders* has something to offer you.

What sets *Lunch with Leaders* apart is its authenticity. These aren't rehearsed and polished corporate stories but candid, unfiltered dialogues that reflect the human side of leadership. The book reminds us that leadership isn't about titles or positions; it's about embracing vulnerability, resilience, and constant growth. Mike Mack's skillful interviewing, combined with the wealth of insights from a diverse range of leaders, makes this book a must-read for those seeking to embark on their own leadership journey or refine their existing leadership skills. It's a reminder that, in the company of great leaders, one can find inspiration, guidance, and the keys to success."

—**Laura Porret**, CPHR, Director, Human Resources
and Leadership Development, JV Driver Group

"I felt as if I was seated at the restaurant table having *Lunch with Leaders* and Mike from the moment I started reading this book. These insightful stories will certainly inspire and motivate anyone who decides to sit at the table with them as well. A meal full of vulnerability, courage, drive, passion, and meaningful purposes served by magnificent writing and storytelling."

—**Eduaro Sguario**, CEO & Cofounder,
LongVision Consulting Brazil

"What struck me most while reading *Lunch with Leaders*, Mike Mack's brilliant new book, was the inspiration ignited through the power of paradox. Whether finding comfort in fear, choosing to be both brave and vulnerable, or remaining calm under pressure, the people profiled in these pages truly demonstrate how often the best leaders are forged through overcoming adversity. A powerful read filled with compelling storytelling and personal perspectives, *Lunch with Leaders* illustrates how a learning mindset helps fuel risk taking and the perpetual pursuit of forward progress."

—**Jennifer Pascoe**, MA (she/her/elle), Vice-President (University Relations) Athabasca University

"The insights that Mike has collected and shared are relevant whether you have five minutes or an hour. I fell into these stories and kept wanting to come back for more."

—**Daniel Rex**, CEO, Toastmasters International

"Through these captivating stories, you'll not only glean valuable business tips but also become engrossed in the unfolding tales of these leaders, eagerly turning page after page to find out what happens next. You'll witness how they navigated a myriad of challenges and seized numerous opportunities along their journey. This book is a must-read for those in pursuit of inspiration and guidance in both the realms of business and leadership."

—**Amir Shami**, P.Eng, MBA, ICD.D, President & CEO, Rotaflow Fire & Utility

"Mike Mack captures the essence of entrepreneurism in this easy to read, insightful and inspiring journey of 12 great leaders. You will see attributes like Risk Appetite, Passion, Tenacity, Purpose, Continuous Learning, Honesty, Authenticity, Ability to Pivot,

Resilience, Creative Solutions and as one of the leaders was quoted "Relentless Forward Progress" as keys to success. This is a must read for any aspiring entrepreneur and leader!"

—**Lorne M. Wight**, President & CEO, Wight Group Ltd.

"With these stories Mike Mack has provided a unique opportunity to learn from those who have already made their mark, providing invaluable insights and guidance for all leaders at all stages of their journey."

—**Teresa Spinelli**, President, Italian Centre Shop

"*Lunch with Leaders* allows the world a small glimpse into Mike's remarkable business network. Entrepreneurs tell the best stories. The contributions from these business leaders will have you cheering and laughing as you see their journeys unfold. Mike's amazing facilitation skills are on display with his ability to ask the right questions and allow these business leaders to tell their captivating stories. In a world where everyone is overselling the positives, *Lunch with Leaders* takes a refreshing look at the struggles and chaos that accompany entrepreneurship. In story telling the logic is retroactive. What seems absurd at first comes together through effective story telling. *Lunch with Leaders* leaves you with the immense satisfaction that you are not alone and that all entrepreneurs face failures that ultimately lead to their success. Anyone that is an entrepreneur or who has thought about starting their own business should read this book."

—**Brian Mack**, MPA, CPA, CMA, Co-Founder, GrowLytics Inc.

"*Lunch with Leaders* is a must-read for any aspiring or evolving entrepreneur. Author, Mike Mack, does a masterful job of drawing out the fascinating back-story from some of Canada's most inspirational business leaders. Like a buffet, *Lunch with Leaders* offers the reader a wide array of themes to savour: motivation and passion, overcoming obstacles, dedication and focus, failure and success, celebration. Though satiated, the reader will be looking forward to more."

—**Rod Burylo**, Director, The Foundation for
the Advancement of Entrepreneurship

"*Lunch with Leaders* lets entrepreneurs reflect back on their own journey while listening to others speak about their journey. Sometimes we are so focused on looking ahead that we don't look back at the accomplishments and hard work that was put in to get the business to where it is today. I certainly saw myself reflecting on the good, the bad and the times you just weren't sure what was going to happen next. Mike from X5 is delivering a great read for all within the pages of the book *Lunch with Leaders*."

—**Sean Schoenberger**, President,
Sunco Communication & Installation

"*Lunch with Leaders* provides an insightful look into the variety of leadership paths and styles that have contributed to leadership success. Each leader's candor and reflection on their own leadership journey is remarkable, providing both perspective and encouragement for current and aspiring leaders. Further, Mike captured these conversations in such an engaging way that it felt like I was at the lunch table with them. This is a must-read for anyone looking for real-life examples of modern leadership."

—**Sheila J. Steger**, C.Dir, Founder and Principal,
Steger Consulting

"Simply reading the title, "*Lunch with Leaders*", my mind raced as I considered the opportunities that those lunches may present. Opportunity to dine with those who have already accomplished what others are freshly encountering. To share stories of success, failure, and even heartache that may engulf either of these outcomes. It's these learnings that can easily go unacknowledged in the hustle and bustle of life, yet most people are kind enough to share. I thoroughly enjoyed the personal stories and shall challenge myself to seek more opportunities for *Lunch with Leaders*."

—**Steve Oslanski**, Partner, Vice President of
Sales & Strategy, Envirotech Geothermal

"I recently had the pleasure of previewing *Lunch with Leaders*. The book takes you on the remarkable journeys of twelve successful entrepreneurs, and I must say, it was an enjoyable read and time well spent. What struck me the most was the authenticity of the journeys, the ups and downs, the challenges and triumphs, and the sheer determination and hard work that define the entrepreneurial spirit. The entrepreneurs that are featured come from diverse backgrounds and industries, and their stories are a testament to the fact that success knows no boundaries. Mike Mack has skillfully authored another book that is not only informative but highly engaging. The journeys are filled with valuable wisdom and insights that leave you with the belief that, with determination and hard work, anything is possible. This is one to put on your reading list for sure."

—**Terry Edwards**, Chief Operating Officer, Decisive Dividend Corporation

"While the business world teeters on the edge of mega takeovers, reputation deterioration, and the reduction of humanity as its backbone, enter bestselling author Mike Mack, author of the new book *Lunch with Leaders*. Mike's book brings inspiration and innovation from these business entrepreneurs reflecting on their real-life narratives.

Through this great collection of interviews, Mike reveals common threads prevalent in these entrepreneurial leaders: all are visionaries, hurdle jumpers, believers and collaborators, but he also reveals their common human threads; personal well-being, self-care, embracing vulnerability, and truly caring about people.

For those seeking positive messages and a sense of hope that the entrepreneurial business community is alive and well, these stories will spark a new energy in your everyday life and bring you hope for the future. One of my favourite quotes that these entrepreneurs embody every day is the following: "Keep going, because you haven't come this far to only come this far". I am honoured to be associated with X5 Management and Mike Mack; congratulations Mike on another fantastic book."

—**Brent Collingwood**, Rotary District Governor 2023-24

"One doesn't have to look far for heartwarming stories of fellow Canadians, who successfully pursued their entrepreneurial callings, and through that, made significant contributions to their community. Mike Mack in his unique and elegant style, brings out the best in these successful entrepreneurs and leaders as they share with us their inspiring, and unique journeys through many challenges which have brought them to where they are today. A "must read" for all aspiring entrepreneurs."

—His Honour, **Dr. Zaheer Lakhani**

"For decades, Mike has used his passion for learning and his love of people to help businesses and leaders be better. Whether through coaching, facilitating, or training, he takes the time to build respect and trust with the people he works with. *Lunch with Leaders* is a great reflection of Mike's ability to share information to inspire people to action. Reading about these 12 remarkable leaders and the challenges they faced along their journeys is such a catalyst for personal growth and learning. Thanks, Mike, for sharing these stories so we can all benefit from their advice and use it to help ourselves get outside of our comfort zones and reach higher."

—**Ashley Morgan** (she/her), MBA, PMP, Chief Marketing and Strategy Officer, Alberta Municipalities

"*Lunch with Leaders* presents the stories that might be shared amongst a group of wonderfully personable and inspirational people over a great meal. It is a truly delightful read, flowing as easily as good conversation. I enjoyed reading about leaders and entrepreneurs, who share openly of their challenges and joys along the road to success. The stories told by each in their own words are insightful while remaining incredibly relatable. I found myself nodding along in agreement with the insights shared and smiling in surprise at the candor. I've read more business and leadership books than I could count, and I have to say that *Lunch with Leaders* stands out of the crowd in its delivery of important thoughts without pretense, buzzwords, or jargon. The stories are shared with the authenticity of real people who have walked the path, vividly describing "behind-the-scenes" details of the growth of their businesses and their learnings along the way. Well done Mike on bringing this project to fruition, it really is special!"

—**Nilam Ram**, CPA, CGA, MBA, Chief
Financial Officer, Stahl Peterbilt

"If you are a leader, or want to become one, pull up a chair and have lunch with these leaders. It's a full menu of stories, lessons, and candid insights from remarkable leaders."

—**Hugh Culver**, Author and 3X founder

"No two leaders, founders or entrepreneurs have the same story. And yet, the consistent themes of resilience, determination, vision, and leadership weave through every story in different ways. Tackling the job of telling those stories is not for the weak of heart. How do you capture the essence of that leader and tell that story and in so doing "share a story that is bigger than yourself"? Mike Mack, in his most recent publication *"Lunch with Leaders"*, has done that with the listening heart, and his own brand of champion leadership that is the essence of his professional life. The inspiration that leaps off these pages is mobilizing and engaging. These Canadians make me proud to be Canadian. They make me humble at the spirit that is at the essence of leadership—and nod in agreement as they discuss their journeys in discovering their leadership identities, their strengths, their challenges, and what brings those talents to the forefront of their lives. Having enjoyed how compelling these stories are, and knowing how many amazing leaders there are like this across Canada, I would just add I can't wait for *Lunch with Leaders* 2.0. Thank you, Mike, for bringing these stories to light!"

—**Yvonne Thevenot**, Independent Consultant, Change Management (Toronto Canada)

"*Lunch with Leaders* captures the entrepreneurial mindset through intimate interviews with small business trailblazers. This succinct book dives into the challenges and successes of entrepreneurship, stressing the importance of resilience and a creative outlook. Ideal for entrepreneurs at any stage, it serves as an inspiring guide, advocating for the adaptable, tenacious thinking vital to business achievement. It's not just stories; it's a concise manual for mindset mastery in the entrepreneurial world."

—**Quentin D. Gardiner**, CPA, CA, CEO, HGA Group,
Partner, HGA Chartered Professional Accountants

"Mike Mack works his magic once more in his fourth book. Aspiring leaders will find themselves captivated from cover to cover as Mike skillfully unravels the journeys of seasoned leaders from various corporate paths, providing invaluable insights for success."

—**Mark Donnelly**, CPA, CA, CFO & VP
Corporate Development, Bits In Glass

"*Lunch with Leaders* distills the essence of leadership through real-world narratives. The stories focus in on the critical junctures that shape a leader, with honest reflections that offer invaluable lessons. The executives' openness provides a ton of mentorship, making the book helpful for both emerging and established leaders.

The range of industries and challenges covered illustrates that while our pivotal moments are deeply personal, the qualities that see us through are universally admired: resilience, adaptability, and courage. The book doubles as a guide, with actionable insights to apply in our own lives.

In essence, this book isn't just about reaching the top—it's about the journey, the climb, and the transformation. A recommended read for anyone on the path to impactful leadership!"

—**Chad Griffiths**, MBA, SIOR, Partner,
Associate Broker, NAI Commercial Real Estate Inc.

"Mike once again continues to have stories and real-world experiences which make my jaw drop. As a business leader with an entrepreneurial fire inside *Lunch with Leaders* provides some exceptional success stories and scenarios where business owners can go from their back against the wall to climbing on top using creativity and out of the box thinking. Business plans are great, until they hit roadblocks or even sink holes. Mike does an outstanding job taking us through these stories of triumphs in the leadership world."

—**Christopher Tonkin**, President, Straightline Motor Group

"When Mike first mentioned his concept for this book to me, I was intrigued. I thought it would be interesting. The final result is WAY beyond interesting! It is a fascinating dive into the minds of entrepreneurial leaders. The stories are filled with incredible insights into both the agony and the joy of leading and building something from the ground up.

It's raw, gritty, funny and real all at once. It's an awesome reminder that as leaders, and just as humans for that matter, we are all a work in process. We are never finished growing. *Lunch with Leaders* can help all of us grow along our journeys and at the same time know that we are not alone in the both the successes we achieve and in the struggles we'll all face along the way."

—**Sean Ryan**, President & CEO, WhiteWater
International Consulting Inc.

"I know this will be an inspirational book that allows readers to learn more about some amazing and successful entrepreneurs and business leaders that you have met and developed relationships with over the years. In the reading so far, I am in awe of the stories that demonstrate, above all, a strong desire to follow one's passion despite venturing into an uncertain outcome. There will be much learning gleaned from these incredible business leaders, and their journeys of success!"

—**Kris Schinke**, MBA, Vice President—
Integration, X5 Management

"The journey of an entrepreneur has the power to inspire. For me, *Lunch with Leaders* is about passion, leadership, risk-taking, staying motivated, hard work, persistence, and balance."

—**Richard A. Wong**, Chief Operating Officer & General
Manager, Chateau Lacombe Hotel Edmonton

"When I look around me, I realize that everything was created by someone and that someone was probably an entrepreneur or if not then they most likely worked for one. One of my favourite things about sitting in my chair at Bond Capital private credit is the many opportunities I have had to interview entrepreneurs like you have done for this book. Any entrepreneurs story is a fascinating account of intrigue and trepidation worthy of the big screen because they embody perseverance in the face of insurmountable odds, calculated risk taking, and passion for turning sources into resources. It has been said that a significant proportion of businesses must close due to lack of funding, bad business decisions, government policies, an economic crisis, a lack of market interest, bullying and or a combination of all of these. I enjoyed the excerpt from Angela Santiago about a lawyer's bullying leading them to improve on their brand name. I was able to reflect wryly on my life's work when Graham Sherman said, "the longest relationship you'll have is with the person, the banker, who loaned you the money." I hope that your book serves as an inspiration for future generations to take their entrepreneurial shot by fearlessly using their time, energy, and resources to create value for others. Here's to celebrating the entrepreneurs that take risk to solve problems so that another's day can be more pleasant. Cheers to you Mike for acting as celebrant."

—**Davis Vaitkunas**, President & Founder, Bond Capital

"Mike Mack hits a home run with *Lunch with Leaders*. His ability to provide leadership lessons while embracing and celebrating the human component is nothing short of amazing. The stories and lessons included in this book are inspiring, thought provoking and motivating. You will see that leadership comes in many forms across all facets of life and business. This is a must read."

—**Jim Ponder**, President & CEO,
Turnkey Strategic Relations, LLC

"From cover to cover, this book is full of entrepreneurial wisdom and inspiration. It brings together a diverse group of leaders and business owners who generously share their captivating stories of the peaks and valleys along their entrepreneurial journeys. Through these stories, readers gain a front-row seat to the challenges and victories faced by individuals from various industries and backgrounds. The collective wisdom within these pages not only offers invaluable lessons on strategy, resilience, and adaptability but also imparts a deeper understanding of the ambition and the drive that it takes to be successful. It's a very motivating read that highlights the power of perseverance and innovation in the world of entrepreneurship, making it a key resource for aspiring and seasoned business professionals."

—**Rachel Hanes**, Chief Operating Officer, HGA Group

"I've known Mike since I was new to the workforce, and since then, he's had a significant influence on my professional growth. In *"Lunch with Leaders"* Mike culminates and shares the stories of Leaders who have similarly influenced him. This approach is so true to Mike—he's there to facilitate growth, generously share insights and act as a cheerleader for the individuals—as he aptly puts it—that he "Likes, Respects and Trusts."

Lunch with Leaders perfectly showcases the humanity, growth, and grit of some genuinely extraordinary leaders. Their stories will inspire new graduates and seasoned professionals alike."

—**Leanne Burrows**, Director, Communications,
Sky Eye Measurement

"When Mike told me that he was starting his newest book *Lunch with Leaders*, I was excited and looking forward to hearing the tales from the folks that he was interviewing as well as Mike's take on what they said. Now that I have had a chance to review a portion of it, my excitement has grown 10X.

Speaking of mastermind leaders, Mike Mack has done it once again with an outstanding book that shares so many insights from so many diverse industries. I am really looking forward to enjoying all of it and seeing what new lessons I will be able to take away from it as well."

—**Jason Desaulniers** CFP, CLU, CIM, CHS, Certified Financial Planner, President of Excalibur Executive Planning Inc./BP Group Solutions

"One of the great things about working with Mike and the X5 Management team is the opportunity to learn from our client base, which comprises a tremendous diversity of experience and circumstance. *Lunch with Leaders* references the stories of both our clients and other leaders at pivotal moments in their professional and personal lives. We are excited to share these stories of learnings along the way—all in support of the goal of inspiring other leaders to be their best selves. For the gifts of their time, wisdom, and most importantly—vulnerability—we are sincerely grateful to everyone profiled in this collection."

—**Anoushka Fernandes**, Vice President of Growth and Development, X5 Management

"*Lunch with Leaders* is a thought-provoking compilation of stories from twelve leaders about the paths they took to create, lead, and grow their successful businesses. Told by the leaders themselves, their stories are compelling, entertaining, and chock-full of inspiration. We can learn from, relate to, or simply enjoy reading about the many challenges and triumphs these entrepreneurs encountered in the evolution of their businesses. Their stories bring smiles and surprises that make this a fun and engaging read.

As they tell their stories, each business owner shares the "why" behind the purpose of their business, how they got started, the decisions they had to make, and the many milestones they achieved. Most importantly—and not surprisingly—their rise to success (and their continued success) rests in part on the strength of the relationships they've built and the understanding of how important it is to surround yourself with people who believe in you, your vision, and your mission. These leaders reveal the grit and determination they embody, while sharing moments of vulnerability and self-doubt along the way. In total, these inspiring stories remind us all of the power and possibility within us and the importance of persistence in the pursuit of our dreams and goals."

—**Leslie Shreve**, Workload Management and Productivity Expert, Founder and CEO, Productive Day®, Creator of Taskology® The Science of Getting Things Done

"*Lunch with Leaders* helps to employ a mindful balance of creativity, promotional growth, and risk psychology. Mike Mack's new book once again exuberates real world triumphs and digests the hard work and dedication that true leaders hold."

—**Gary Wood**, Service Manager, Stahl Peterbilt

"*Lunch with Leaders* provides insight into the journey of influential business leaders as they share their candid and authentic personal experiences. This collection is not just a celebration of success but a testament to resilience and humility, offering invaluable insights that transcend the boundaries of business. Mike Mack's *Lunch with Leaders* is a source of inspiration for aspiring entrepreneurs and seasoned professionals alike, seeking inspiration from the lived experiences of those who have navigated the business landscape with both passion and perseverance."

—**Melissa Smart** (she/her), Vice President of Ticket Service & Operations, OEG Sports & Entertainment

"Mike is a fixture of our local business community and curator of leadership wisdom. This collection of first-person accounts will invigorate budding entrepreneurs, re-assure owners of growing businesses, and reveal new truths to those who have "made it". As the owner of a growing business, I am re-assured to see a small part of myself in these stories and, importantly, a glimpse of what I would like to become. *Lunch with Leaders* is a welcome break in the daily grind of business to re-ignite your passion!"

—**Jason A. Banack**, Principal, HGA Law

"Mike Mack's book, *Lunch with Leaders* brings the reader to the table while these conversations are unfolding. The book allows the reader to peer through a keyhole into what makes entrepreneurs successful with all the setbacks along the way. A common thread throughout *Lunch with Leaders* is these successful leaders all had role models they wanted to emulate or not let down. The book also illustrates the small nuances such as being curious and not accepting "no for an answer" that separated these exceptional leaders from individuals that conceded to the status quo. Mikes' book is an inspirational look at how today's business leaders have overcome everyday challenges and have learned to grow into multifaceted leaders that we all can look up to."

—**Joe Gagliardi**, FCPA, FCMA, ICD.D, Managing Partner
Recruitment Partners Inc. Edmonton | Calgary

"Mike's latest book is full of insightful anecdotes from many of Alberta's top business leaders. With each chapter, we have "lunch" and learn valuable knowledge from decades of leadership. An essential addition to any business bookshelf!"

—**Justin LaRocque**, CEO, River City Leaders Forum (RCLF)

"Mike Mack is at it again with his fourth book, *Lunch with Leaders*. This time, Mike Mack brings together a collection of leaders who discuss and share their individual road maps to success, motivations, and ever-constant change; all of it broken down into bite-size chunks, making for an enjoyable and rewarding read. *Lunch with Leaders* is an engaging book taken from the perspective of a dozen different leaders sharing an equal number of approaches to success—all relatable to anyone in business."

—**Jody Young**, General Manager, Lethbridge Country Club

"This excellent book is very easy to read while illustrating many difficult challenges we all face in our businesses and personal lives in the real world today. The real treat for me was being inspired by their honest authentic portrayal of their pivotal moments and the processes they went through to decide which new pathway was the one to bring new leadership skills and success not only to their business but to themselves personally. Mike has selected entrepreneurs for this book that give you truly authentic candid stories. The way they talk about their vulnerabilities helped me feel that I am not alone. They gave me hope and courage to follow their lead in pivoting to a new path that can drive great success in organizing as they did."

—**Neil Wilkinson**, Past International President, Toastmasters International

"Having the good fortune of knowing Mike in a professional capacity since the spring of 2011, I can appreciate the many pivotal moments that I have experienced in my own leadership journey over the years. Some good, some very difficult! *Lunch with Leaders* is a must read for any leader who wants to look through the leadership lens of others who have experienced challenges, setbacks and had the resilience to keep going. Their stories of grit, will, and belief, should inspire all of us to face our next challenge or leverage an opportunity with the determination and desire to protect, or improve our business and team's future reality."

—**Brent Lawrence**, Director of Parts & Service Operations, Stahl Peterbilt

"It was fascinating to read the back stories of these amazing leaders, as they retell firsthand, their rugged journeys to success and ongoing perseverance. What the outside world often only sees is the successful business as it is today. Mike does a great job at revealing the candid, fascinating and often vulnerable back story in the years before the success.

I believe we are all leaders in our own lives and the work, or job we have. As Mike dives into the lunch, he asks excellent questions, and the stories unfold organically. They provide a roadmap for living and are transferable skills to those of us who want to be successful both personally and professionally. Each story is unique but if you peel away the onion, you can find the invisible thread that links all of them. I encourage you to find the thread that speaks to you. A great read that can be done in small doses or an afternoon binge, you decide."

—**Bonita Lehmann**, Channel Sales Manager, Canada, Formlabs

"Too often, we read success stories only seeing the 'highlight reels' and results and we miss the pursuit of the journey. Mike Mack gets to the real heart of these leaders as people, and further explores the depth of their whole journey while unpacking, in intimate detail, how they've arrived where they are today. You will get candid stories of their struggles, decision-making crossroads, and journey of unrelenting perseverance, which have served as some of their most vulnerable moments as leaders and humans. Ultimately, Mack highlights how these experiences profoundly shaped their authenticity and success as leaders. This collection of human stories brings forward so much to consider. Enjoy each person Mike captures here."

—**Wayne Fraser**, Managing Director and Head, Corporate Client Group (Alberta and Territories), RBC

"We have worked with Mike Mack for many years now; his approach is unique and truly dives into understanding entrepreneurship. His laser focus on helping drive businesses to be successful while overcoming challenges and obstacles has brought together a wonderful combination of true story's. His new book really is a *must* read, as it takes you through 12 truthful journeys from real life business leaders and what they had dealt with including the ups and downs of each of their situations. *Lunch with Leaders* is a fantastic read and should be a priority if you are an entrepreneur or striving to be one!"

—**Denis Dale**, President, Bob Dale Gloves & Imports

"Many times, as entrepreneurs, our tanks are empty. Lunch with Leaders is a book that will refuel all of us. To read others' journeys and struggles in authentic and heartfelt ways, it reminds us it's not easy to be an entrepreneur, a family member, a friend, and a healthy person. However, it's not impossible! With each interview we get to choose how each story will impact us, inspire us and refuel us. Thank you, Mike Mack, for assembling great leaders and sharing their stories."

—**Hubert Lau**, President, TrustBIX Inc., TSX.V: TBIX, OTCQB: TBIXF

Lunch
with
Leaders

REAL STORIES
OF PIVOTAL MOMENTS
FOR TODAY'S EXECUTIVE

Mike Mack

WINDERMERE
PRESS

LUNCH WITH LEADERS
Real Stories of Pivotal Moments for Today's Executive
First Edition

ISBN 978-1-962341-21-9 *Hardcover*
978-1-962341-20-2 *Paperback*
978-1-962341-23-3 *Ebook*

This book is about leaders that have been through the struggles and joys of their personal and professional lives, and it was an obvious choice for me to dedicate my fourth book to my late father-in-law, Hugo Lehmann. He was an entrepreneur, loving family man, and someone who made a difference in his community. He passed away in October 2023 at the age of 92.

I am grateful for every moment that we spent together, and the wisdom and lessons learned from each conversation.

Contents

x x x

Foreword

What an honor it is to write the foreword for this book by the author and my long-time friend, Mike Mack.

Thirty-seven years ago, when Mike and I were just starting out in our banking careers, we often shared our thoughts on how our teams were doing and the next steps we wanted to take. Although our experiences were limited, our ambitions were plentiful. We had a lot in common, especially in terms of growing our families and careers, but our most significant bond was our belief in finding and living our purpose. For Mike, this belief led him to develop an impressive leadership practice, culminating in the founding of X5 Management and investing in the next generation of leaders nationwide.

Mike has a unique talent for bringing out the best in people and helping them realize their full potential. He's also a gifted storyteller, holding the belief that we can learn from each other's experiences. Fortunately for all of us, in *Lunch with Leaders*, Mike shares twelve impactful stories that will inspire and motivate you to enhance your own leadership journey.

In writing this book, Mike connected with leaders from a variety of industries, demographics, and cultures. Despite their differences, they all share one thing in common: they are living their purpose. Many of them began their careers under unexpected circumstances, not following traditional paths, but instead carving their own. Some encountered a problem and sought to solve it, while others took risks on something they believed in. Throughout this book, they recount the rough lessons they learned, their failures, and their triumphant successes. You will hear them articulate what purpose means to them and how it acts as a driving force in their businesses and careers. They each have incredible stories to share, and thanks to Mike's innate ability to bring people together, you'll feel as though you're sitting beside each leader as they personally recount the beginnings of their leadership journey and how it led them to their current positions.

Whether you are an experienced leader or just starting out, I am confident that you will find a wealth of inspiration in this book and in each leader's story. I challenge you to reflect after each chapter on how you would handle similar leadership scenarios and how you would use your life's purpose as a guiding light.

And finally, to Mike: congratulations on your fourth book in just seven years—a truly remarkable achievement! Thank you for your steadfast commitment to leadership and for helping others discover and harness their talents. This book is a testament to how every entrepreneur can lead by example, positively influencing others through your purpose.

—**CURTIS STANGE**
President and CEO, ATB Financial

Introduction

If you are a business leader, owner, or entrepreneur, this book is for you.

Have you ever felt like your business challenges are only unique to you?

You are not alone; no entrepreneur is. Many other leaders and entrepreneurs have experienced the same challenges, along with the highs and lows of business leadership.

In *Lunch with Leaders*, I had the distinct pleasure of sitting down with twelve top executives who share their wisdom and insights that they have learned about what it takes to run a successful business. They experienced challenges, setbacks and had to get back up and be resilient to fight another day. We get to experience real stories of their pivotal moments and ideally apply it to today's struggles or challenges in our own business.

It is my strong belief that their very candid honesty and vulnerability will lend invaluable insights and perspective to your own business journey. and hopefully give you the courage and strength to keep on, keeping on when times get tough.

And they *will* get tough, sometimes when we least expect it. As a business leader or entrepreneur there are days when you are on top of the world, and it seems like everything in your business is running like a well-oiled machine. What a feeling as you are building momentum, and the future looks bright. But business reality rears its ugly head, and just like that, you have a major crisis or huge disruption in your business.

This could be a valued client who is threatening to leave, and the impact on your topline would be catastrophic. A major business partner conflict leads to the dissolution of the partnership, and now everything is in disarray, and the future is uncertain. You suffer the untimely death of a key person in your business or a close family member. The world experiences a black swan event, and you literally don't know which way to turn. Your business is faced with a lawsuit that puts a tight grip on your operations, and emotionally, it cripples the forward direction of your business plans and growth, and challenges your infrastructure. Several top employees are poached by your competition, and your bench strength is stripped so lean that the vulnerability of your business is exposed and creates massive risk to growth. Your relationship with your bank is strained, and they continue to tighten the reins on your access to financing, and growth capital is tight. You hit a wall and don't know which way to turn.

In times like these, great leaders decide how they will navigate through these pivotal moments in their business. *Should I do this? Should I make this key decision?* There is no decision that gives you absolute certainty, but someone needs to make the decision, and not making any decision is a ticking time bomb.

Most leaders and entrepreneurs are visionaries and see the big picture, which is a future imagined condition of their organization. They are open to many options and are generally very adventurous, and they are willing to explore what's possible. They think longer-term and want their future reality for their team and their business to be bigger, better, stronger, and faster. What's possible? Who wouldn't want a bigger future reality in business? That's what visionary leaders and entrepreneurs do, as it gets them up in the morning, every single day, even on weekends and vacations.

But that bigger vision and future reality comes with challenges and obstacles, and at times you don't know which way to turn. You want the playbook and a way to listen and learn from others who have been there, done that.

You don't have to always reinvent the wheel. The leaders whose stories fill these pages have led the way through the dark times of business and guided their ship to the light. Listening and learning from others can sometimes be a game-changer.

In *Lunch with Leaders*, you will learn how great leaders have navigated the rough waters of business, from tragedy due to the loss of loved ones to economic downturns that make you think: *How the hell did they get through that?* You are invited to sit at the same table with highly successful leaders and entrepreneurs, committed advocates, and award-winning business executives as they explore in depth the events that paved the way for their success. Discover the rules they live by and how they pivoted their way through struggles and major adversity.

As an entrepreneur for 17+ years after starting my business, X5 Management, a Training, Coaching, and Consulting firm, I have had the unique privilege of sitting at the table with many leaders on a daily and weekly basis. While I am there to help them and their teams align for a bigger future, I too get to learn from them. I can't help it as we develop and build deeply rooted, trusting relationships over time. I gravitate towards entrepreneurs and business leaders as I realize that over the years, I can relate on so many levels.

I have also discovered along the way that my own business wasn't without adversity and challenges over the years, and I too had to pivot and navigate choppy waters, but fortunately, I arrived safely ashore, until the next time when I am faced with an unexpected challenge.

Back in 2007, I was in the early stages of building my business, and while I had many connections, they weren't with very many senior leaders, influencers, or entrepreneurs with whom I was really close or connected. I often thought, wouldn't it be great to sit down over lunch and just learn from these successful and inspiring leaders who have done so many things? For the record, the many things were not just about making money, but how they supported the community, their travel, the various non-profit boards they served on, the associations they were part of, lessons learned, and so much more.

One of the most impactful books I read at that time was *Never Eat Alone: And Other Secrets to Success, One Relationship at a Time*, by Keith Ferrazzi and Tahl Raz. The concept of the book is a guide on how to make meaningful connections and leverage relationships to accomplish your goals and help others accomplish theirs. The primary strategy in the book, "Never Eat Alone", encourages you to stop eating *lunch* by yourself, and instead use that time to connect with other people.

Little did I know at the time that this aspiration, coupled with my own entrepreneurial journey, would one day be the catalyst to write *Lunch with Leaders*!

I consider myself blessed and fortunate to have had the opportunity to work with and build relationships with many great leaders and entrepreneurs in my professional life. While some of them have become friends and clients, many have been key centres of influence in my life. That was a major factor in connecting with the leaders featured in the chapters ahead.

The vision and purpose of writing and publishing this book, my fourth over the past seven years, was to share the wisdom, insights, and journey of these resilient and seasoned leaders.

While all the profiled leaders are based in Canada (many from Alberta), their lessons are globally universal. I believe you will find the stories to be incredible, insightful, engaging, and at times, heartbreaking, all in one.

While I have enjoyed a lunch or beverage with many of them over the years, the world of virtual connection (Teams/Zoom) allowed me the opportunity to sit with each of them, ask several questions, and just listen to them, learn about their journey and story, and try to capture the essence of their words on paper in such a way as to make it a valuable, yet an enjoyable reading experience for all who decide to get a copy of my book and sit down to read it. As you read, you'll notice that each chapter is structured in an interview format to capture their story in their own words. Every chapter has many great takeaways for anyone who aspires to be a leader or entrepreneur, or if you have been one for 20+ years, there is something for all of you.

One thing that I am confident about—whether you read for three hours nonstop or read one chapter at a time, you will gain from the lessons learned from these leaders, and I want to thank them in advance as you begin reading the book. Without their decision to participate in the book, invest the time to speak with me, the experiences and wisdom that you are about to read would not have been possible.

Like any book, you get to decide what you will learn and take away. I encourage you to think about The One Thing that you can glean and implement from each chapter that you read.

There are hundreds of years of wisdom that comes from these leaders, all of whom have faced real business challenges and enjoyed great success.

Enjoy their incredible stories!

1

Innovative Leaders are the Most Vulnerable
Shawn Kanungo and Disruptive Innovation

OW DOES ONE TRANSITION FROM ACCOUNT-
ing to becoming a bestselling author and a globally
recognized speaker? Shawn Kanungo takes us on
his transformative journey, highlighting the moments that have
defined his path.

I had the privilege of meeting Shawn Kanungo in 2017
through my involvement with ACG (Association for Corporate
Growth) in Edmonton when I served as the Chapter President,
and we had Shawn as one of our keynote speakers. He was

excellent and really impacted our audience in a thought-provoking way. We maintained contact and I followed Shawn's professional journey with great interest as he continued to impact the business community with his insights and very energized presentations.

I reached out to Shawn and asked him, "We don't get to talk to each other very often and I hold you in very high regard. I asked you to be in my new book, and without hesitation you said 'yes'. Why?"

"Mike, I think you are definitely somebody that is a leader, a community leader within the city and beyond. I have a lot of respect for you and how you carry yourself. And I see how much you care about individuals, and I will give my time to people that care for others all day long. I want to be there for you because of how you've treated me and others. And I think that's a testament to what you've built and the reputation that you've built, which is unbelievable."

A BIG CHANGE

One of the pivotal moments in my life occurred shortly after university when my father unexpectedly passed away in April 2008. He was the founder of Kanungo and Associates, an accounting firm boasting over 200 clients. Overnight, I found myself leading a company that I had no idea how to run.

This moment forced me to reconfigure my entire mindset and life. The day after my father's passing, I walked into his office, scared out of mind, but ready for the challenge. I had to swiftly learn not only the intricacies of managing a business but also what it meant to step into adulthood and leadership. Honestly, it was a stark reminder that life is short. From that moment on, I committed to living every single day like it was my last. Even today, I'm fuelled by that same hunger, feeling as though my journey has just begun.

In 2006, I began my journey with Deloitte within Accounting. After obtaining my CA, I swiftly transitioned to Management Consulting in 2009, recognizing it as a career that best suited my talents and interested. However, another significant turning point in my career came when I ventured into the hot mobile app universe. As the Apple App Store's popularity surged, some friends and I co-founded a mobile app company. We also started a creative film group. We developed a bunch of consumer-focused apps, immersing me into the entire world of customer experience, user interface, and digital innovation.

This hands-on experience became my real-world MBA. Even while still with Deloitte, the insights I gained from these ventures allowed me to spearhead initiatives in Deloitte's digital, innovation, and technology sectors. Within the firm, my endeavors became synonymous with 'innovation'. I don't even really know what that meant. Colleagues across the firm recognized the work, and somebody from the real innovation team said, "While everyone's talking about innovation, Shawn Kanungo's teams are the ones actualizing it." From incorporating novel technologies to pioneering methodologies, we were at the forefront.

My influence within Deloitte's innovation sphere grew, not just nationally, but on global projects as well. I also started to create buzz around my public speaking engagements and digital content. By 2018, I realized the magnitude of the impact I could create independently. This realization spurred me to establish my own firm, where I could advise organization and cultivate my personal brand. It showed me that I could create my own book, The Bold Ones, and an accompanying streaming special on Apple TV and Amazon Prime Video.

AN ACCOUNTANT THAT DOESN'T
THINK LIKE AN ACCOUNTANT

While I briefly dabbled in accounting, it was management consulting where I truly found my stride. Though my stint in accounting was short-lived, my decade in consulting felt like a century of hands-on experience. Being in one of the most influential consulting firms accelerated my professional growth exponentially. I felt like one year was ten years of experience. Strategy consulting just pushes you in a ton of different environments, industries, and uncharted waters.

At the same time, on the side, I started to do more speaking engagements, I honed my skills in presentation, persuasion, and influence. True strategy isn't about devising a plan; it's about convincing others. While innovative ideas are thrown around easily, the real challenge is actually steering stakeholders down a particular path.

Effective presentation, be it virtual or in-person, goes beyond mere storytelling. It's an intricate dance of graphics, presence, design aesthetics, performance and more. I think my creativity, particularly in crafting striking visuals and graphics, added another layer to my toolbox.

Being on stage is a multifaceted endeavor. This understanding led us to the Myer Horowitz Theatre in Edmonton, where we've staged over 200 productions. The theater's design aesthetic isn't just about looking good; it's about evoking a feeling. It's the reason why when we shot the special for Apple TV and Prime Video, we wanted to make look beautiful and awe-inspiring.

THE IMPORTANCE OF BRAND EQUITY

Many perceive me as a strategist and thought leader. If I meet someone new—for instance, sitting next to someone on a flight—I usually say "I'm in consulting" to avoid delving into specifics. At my core, I am in the business of helping others creating value through unexpected ways. My mission is to change people's lives, and I realized I can do that the best through content—it could be through my talks, podcasts, streaming specials, or books. I realized that it's the greatest source of brand equity that you can build.

With strong personal brand equity, opportunities multiply. It's not uncommon for businesses to approach me with offers of shares or equity. This brand strength also facilitates connections with incredible organizations and global leaders. I'm biased, but

I think building brand equity is the safest thing you can do for your career.

RECOGNITION

One accolade that stands out for me was from Forbes in early 2021, naming me "The Best Virtual Keynote Speaker I've Ever Seen." This acknowledgment caught me off guard. Kevin Kruse, the article's author and a notable figure in the leadership domain, stumbled upon my work and grew intrigued. Following an interview with him, I was pretty uncertain about the article's direction, half-expecting it to be a feature of other speakers. The final piece's focus was both humbling and insane. It was a nod not just to my efforts, but also to my dedicated team who were helping me put those productions together—BAD Films, Moh and Mazen Mahfouz.

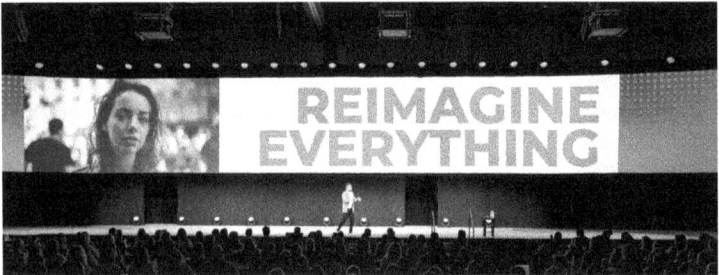

What amplified its significance was the global recognition. It's really an odd phenomenon, but when you recognized outside your own city, it carries more weight.

THE IMPACT OF THE PANDEMIC

The spring of 2020 presented another incredible pivot point for many due to the global pandemic. Fortunately, I had a head start with video already because I've been doing it for so long. Why? Because video is the greatest medium when it comes to story-telling, influence, and persuasion. In a digital realm, there's no better medium than video.

So, when the world transitioned to a digital-first approach, I felt it was a home game. Sure, the pandemic caught me off guard, much like everyone else. My speaking engagements came to an abrupt halt, as did my advisory client interactions. But adversity often breeds innovation. I rallied my production and posed a challenge: "Have any of you ever livestreamed?" Met with a chorus of "No's," I knew we were diving into uncharted territory. However, my goal was clear: "We need to produce the best livestream anyone has ever seen."

Innovation, to me, is about setting oneself apart, about differentiation. In this ever-evolving digital landscape, the only boundary is the one we set for ourselves. If it wasn't for the pandemic, I would have never been able to shoot a special to get a book deal, launch a special on Apple TV and Prime Video. It was my launchpad.

DEALING WITH HARDSHIP AND ADVERSITY

To me, the most impactful leaders embody a blend of innovation and vulnerability. It's the willingness to lay all cards on the table, admitting, "I don't have all the answers." Whether it was stepping into my father's firm or navigating the complexities of strategy consulting, humility, authenticity, and genuineness have always been my guiding principles. Leadership isn't about always having the right answer. It's about building respect by empowering others and guiding them down chosen paths. Vulnerability has been instrumental in my journey, enhancing my credibility and approachability.

Leading strategy innovation at Deloitte further solidified my belief: when you align individuals with their passions, anyone can be unstoppable.

INSPIRING PASSION IN YOUR PEOPLE

Even today, I advocate for hiring individuals with a passion, and it often shows up in their side hustles. For instance, I once hired a woman with a passion for photography. Her Instagram account showcased her impeccable taste, design sensibility, and aesthetic acumen. Aligning her skills with roles in human-centred design, customer experience, or user experience was a no-brainer. She ended up doing her Masters in the field from Harvard and working at Google!

Similarly, I encountered another mentee deeply passionate about blockchain. Recognizing his incredible passion, my goal became clear: integrate him into blockchain projects. Once the pieces fit, he was absolutely unstoppable.

To me, effective leadership hinges on the ability to discern individual strengths and passions. When a leader can align an individual's purpose with the organization's goals, they unlock an unparalleled level of creativity.

TO REINVENT OR NOT TO REINVENT, THAT IS THE QUESTION

It's truly remarkable to witness the vast array of organizations and individuals who have redefined their approach, adapting and evolving in response to changing circumstances.

Take Walmart, for example. I collaborated closely with them when they were launching a new financial card in Canada. What struck me was their proactive approach to disruption. They recognized the need to overhaul their entire approach to traditional financial services to reinvent the process. In a move unlike I've ever seen, they assembled the most diverse cross-functional teams, brainstorming innovative solutions—from crypto to partnerships with influencers and creators. Here was a global industry leader, with the world at its disposal, signaling a readiness to reinvent and disrupt for the sake of exponential growth.

I firmly believe that the pandemic played a pivotal role in this shift in mindset. It served as a global catalyst, signaling that the rules of the game had irrevocably changed. Remember, at its core, every organization is a collective of individuals. The pandemic underscored the need for change, and even for a giant like Walmart, this realization was transformative.

What's truly noteworthy is that those who embraced change, who reimagined their operations, not only thrived but also seemed more content. While I don't claim expertise in happiness, I believe people become happier after they pushed boundaries.

PUSHING BOUNDARIES

In our rapidly evolving world, complacency is perhaps the most dangerous place to me. Mediocrity, especially in these times, is like walking a tightrope over a chasm of irrelevance. The pandemic underscored a crucial lesson: those who aren't malleable, adaptable, and willing to venture into the unknown risk fading into obscurity.

While I recognize the importance of focus, I honestly believe in the need to constantly push boundaries. It's essential to cultivate resilience, to embrace adaptability, and to relentlessly acquire new skills.

As an innovator, anticipation is key. The digital wave, which we've long seen coming, underscores the need to continually upgrade our skillset and mindset. I'm constantly immersing myself in cutting-edge technologies like Generative AI and Web3, dedicating a significant portion of my time to understanding, connecting, and creating in this new universe. After all, as these technologies herald the next age of innovation, why wouldn't I spend my time dedicating hours to it?

THE BOLD ONES

Released in December 2022, my debut book, *The Bold Ones: Innovate and Disrupt to Become Truly Indispensable* delves into the power of disruption at the individual level. This is for the creator, the founder, the entrepreneur, the manager, the new grad, the tinkerer and the lost. Further amplifying this message, an accompanying streaming special was launched on Apple TV and Prime in August 2023.

At its core, *The Bold Ones* unravels the essence of what it means to possess the DNA of a disruptor. It showcases trailblazers—spanning history to the present—who have dared to challenge the norm, reshaping the direction of entire industries. My intrigue isn't with those who merely excel in their domains; rather, it's with the game-changers, those who dare to rewrite the playbook. That's what disruptors do.

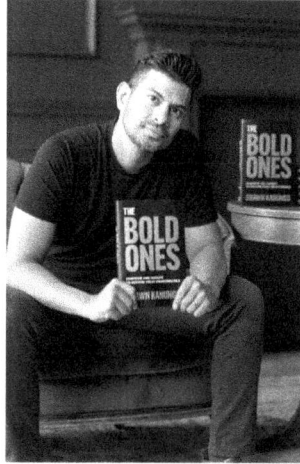

Throughout my life, I've been captivated by the concept of disruption and the individuals who redefine the status quo. I believe there is this massive power shift from institutions to individuals, and I felt compelled to explore the makings of a true disruptor. I believe we're standing on the cusp of a revolution—an era where individuals will spearhead revolutionary changes across every single industry.

My drive to write the book and special were not money or brand, but deeply personal. As I forged my own path, crafting a brand identity through content creation and public speaking, I experienced firsthand what this power shift was all about it.

The Bold Ones is my call-out to illuminate this journey, offering readers insights into how they too can harness the power of disruption. Choosing a traditional publisher and streaming platforms was a conscious decision. I wanted this content to reach new audiences globally. *The Bold Ones* is more than just a book and a special; it's a testament to my beliefs and aspirations. It's a movement for the dreamers and changemakers.

DEFINITION OF SUCCESS

At its core, success, for me, is about the richness of close, intimate relationships and being encircled by incredible individuals. While family and friends form the bedrock of this, from a professional standpoint, my mission is to help others create value in the world. It's about influencing a vast audience, elevating their lives, and helping them feel more empowered.

This drive fuels my passion for content and inspired my foray into writing. While personal interactions are invaluable, there's an undeniable power in disseminating ideas widely. I genuinely feel as though I'm on the precipice of something monumental – I'm just starting.

KEY TRAITS AND QUALITIES OF GREAT ENTREPRENEURS AND LEADERS

While I may be biased, I wholeheartedly believe that leaders who dare to disrupt their own worlds are the epitome of greatness.

These are the visionaries who, despite being already successful, have the audacity to rethink and reinvent. In my view, the most impactful leaders are those who wear vulnerability as a badge of honor. Their focus is unwavering, their vision clear and singular, yet they are perpetually curious! They immerse themselves in reading, listening, experimenting, and exploring what's next, and they're hungry to *create* the future.

I have a particular admiration for hands-on leaders, those who dive deep into the trenches. It's the leader who says, "I devoted my weekend to collaborating on this pioneering Blockchain, Web3 project," that truly captivates me. Their insatiable curiosity and relentless drive embody the essence of innovation and disruption.

MISSED OPPORTUNITIES

In retrospect, I believe I didn't embrace failure early enough. I cared too much about what others thought. I looked for praise from people above me even though they would be long dead before they truly understood my impact.

The true essence of growth and progress lies in facing setbacks and learning from them. Had I been more in tune with this philosophy during my university years or the early stages of my career, I would've perhaps been more adventurous. I didn't really awaken until the passing of my father. Until then, my journey mirrored that of any typical individual in their early twenties. I recognize that period as a missed opportunity, a chapter where I could've been bolder.

However, I view my path as still unfolding. There's an insatiable hunger within me, a drive to seize every opportunity and delve deep into the incredible possibilities that lie ahead. I literally wrote the book on boldness, so I have to be an example of it!

MY FUTURE MISSION

My aspirations stretch beyond of what I've built today. My mission is to help others create value in their worlds, and I believe the best way to do that is to create a brand and media company that can help scale globally.

On a more personal note, I envision a life where I can introduce my three children to the beauty of the world. I want them to understand how to face uncertainty and challenges, learn how to fail and build deep meaningful relationships.

Furthermore, I'm deeply drawn to philanthropy, especially in the realm of education. Empowering individuals across the globe with the tools for a brighter future. The greatest opportunity for disruption is in education.

When my journey concludes, I hope the world remembers me as someone that was always there for his family and friends. I hope they recall a man who responded, who was always present, and who prioritized others. I want my legacy to be about reinvention and evolution—a someone that was always pursuing his passions.

FINAL THOUGHTS

The concept of a "disruptor" often carries a negative connotation. Yet, at its core, it signifies the ability to challenge the status quo, alter one's own path, and potentially reshape the journey of others. True leadership is not just about personal transformation but about acting as a beacon, illuminating the way for others, even from a distance.

The most impactful leaders have a narrative that resonates, inspiring others to chase their own dreams. We often underestimate the profound influence we can wield. That's the beauty of the people you're curating in this book. By weaving together diverse tales of leadership, you're creating a tapestry of inspiration. My hope is that a reader might stumble upon a chapter—any chapter—and feel a spark, driving them to embark on their own transformative journey. I just hope you loved this one!

Shawn Kanungo is a globally recognized innovation strategist and best-selling author. He previously spent twelve years at Deloitte working closely with leaders to better plan for the opportunities associated with disruptive innovation.

He has been recognized as Edify's Top 40 Under 40. In 2021, he was named in *Forbes* as the "Best Virtual Keynote Speaker I've Ever Seen".

Shawn's content on innovation has garnered millions of views, respectively across LinkedIn, TikTok, YouTube & Facebook.

In August 2023, he released a documentary film on Apple TV+ and Amazon Prime that focuses on his debut book, *The Bold Ones*. The bestselling book offers a playbook for individuals to become bolder to push their careers and companies forward. *The Bold Ones* has been touted as one of McKinsey's top decision-making books for leaders.

2

Fear Is a Choice
Chuck Sanders and
JV Driver Group

H OW DOES A GAS JOCKEY-TURNED-FIREFIGHTER
decide to become an accountant, then eventually go
on to lead a billion-dollar business?

I am delighted to share the journey of Chuck Sanders, CEO
of JV Driver Group (a private investment company). Chuck grew
up on Vancouver Island in a blue-collar town and evolved to
become a highly respected and empowering leader driving business operations around the globe.

GETTING MY START

I was born in Alberta, but when I was two, my parents moved
to Vancouver Island, where I grew up and began my career. We

lived in a small town called Shawnigan Lake. Growing up in a logging and farming community, I did typical small-town activities. From the age of 10, I worked in various blue-collar jobs, including dairy farms, gas stations, land development, and excavation. These experiences taught me a lot about leadership, especially what not to do. I observed the small-town farmers, contractors, and developers I worked for closely. While I didn't particularly love the work, it was rewarding at the time, and I earned as I had hoped for my age. However, I was more intrigued by how they managed their businesses, interacted with their employees, and addressed various challenges.

Over the years, I observed my dad's business interactions and leadership style closely. I worked with my dad in his business during my high school and college years. We also served as firefighters together, where he was the long-time local fire chief. With a 46-year career in the fire service, alongside managing several businesses, my dad showcased exemplary leadership skills. I had a firsthand experience of his leadership style, learning both what to emulate and what to avoid. One significant takeaway was understanding the importance of treating people with respect, empowerment, and influence as cornerstones for effective execution.

From him, I also learned the essence of approaching business with an investor's mindset. To grow a business, one needs a capitalistic perspective to focus on working "on" the business rather than just "in" it.

Eventually, my journey led me to become an accountant. In public practice, I noticed a shortage of capitalistic drive in professional services, which wasn't appealing. I wanted the opposite: to harness the collective power in a business to generate returns and profits. The limitation of public practice lies in the finite hours a partner and their team can commit. It seemed like a pretty tough way to earn a living, with so many constraints. I started thinking about what else I wanted to do in the future—and I immediately thought of being an investor.

In 1998, I was three years out of high school working toward my CPA and I had the good fortune of being introduced to JV Driver, a client of the firm. I had observed their growth, from when they had only six employees to becoming a regional industrial contractor. By 2005, I had left public practice and joined JV Driver relocating back to Alberta. My career with JV Driver started as part of the finance team and eventually I became the Chief Financial Officer, a position I held for over a decade. We frequently discussed succession plans, and I was often seen as a potential successor for the CEO position, following our founder.

However, in August 2015, due to a tragic event in our founder's life — the loss of one of his children — I unexpectedly assumed both the CEO and CFO roles. This period was especially challenging, as the person we lost had been someone we all knew and worked with. Beyond the personal grief, we faced significant business challenges, including an energy industry downturn in Alberta that led to its eventual collapse. Filling the shoes of our founder, who effectively stepped back on that fateful day, was daunting.

As time passed, it became clear that the energy industry was not rebounding. Our mainstay, industrial construction, was no longer sustainable. After several tough discussions and decisions, we decided to shut that segment down, stabilizing our construction business and pivoting our strategy towards diversification into various businesses, industries, and regions. This shift proved beneficial, transforming us from an operationally focused entity to a more investor-centric one at the holding company level. Today, we still have a strong growing and vibrant construction business and are invested in a variety of other industries, distinct from construction and our origins in industrial services, energy, and forestry.

PIVOTAL MOMENTS

We were facing some tough decisions essential for our business's survival. At that time, our workforce ranged between 4,000 to 4,500 employees, many of whom were engaged in the construction sector, especially industrial construction. It was a difficult choice, but we reduced this number to almost nothing over time. Today, while we no longer employ anyone in the industrial sector, our overall staff count remains between 3,500 to 4,000, spread across various industries and regions. Our revenue stands comparable to our 2015 figures. However, what once constituted 70 to 80% of our revenue, nearing a billion dollars, has shifted. We've diversified and now draw about a billion dollars in revenue from multiple businesses. This transformation leveraged our longstanding diversification strategy, prompting us to delve deeper into this strategy.

Reflecting on 2015, I remember the overwhelming weight of the situation. I often questioned whether I was the right fit for the challenges that lay ahead. Admittedly, I made mistakes, but with unwavering support and introspection, I mustered the strength to confront our challenges head-on. I realized that if not me, then who? And if not now, then when? Embracing the role, I understood that perfection wasn't attainable, but decisive leadership was imperative. The responsibility rested on me and our executive team to steer the company forward.

A CALLING TO LEAD

Reflecting on my journey, Mike, it's clear that leadership has always been my calling. Whether in the fire service, my prior career in public practice, or any other endeavor, my innate drive and the support of others consistently propelled me into leadership roles. Rather than striving to be the best firefighter or accountant, I recognized that leadership was my true strength. I realized, "There's something here. I should focus on where my natural abilities lie and how I can add value." With this understanding, I recognized that as a leader, there are moments when you have to just step up and take the lead. That's the nature of being a leader!

DIFFICULT CONVERSATIONS

From my viewpoint, a key approach to handling situations is by embracing one of the four agreements: "Don't take things personally." While I strive to uphold this, I'm not always successful. However, we all have the power to choose our reactions. When we observe something, it elicits thoughts and emotions. At that moment, we can decide, "How do I want to feel about this observation?" Especially during tough conversations, we're faced with choices. We can opt for curiosity, seeking to understand the full situation, or acknowledge that we might not be prepared for the conversation.

Recognizing these aspects and exercising the power of choice in our reactions can make a significant difference. Many tend to interpret others' actions and add unnecessary subtext to conversations, which can cloud the real issues at hand. I aim to navigate away from such pitfalls. The key is not to take things personally, avoid reading too much into observations, and approach discussions with curiosity, calmness, and devoid of excessive emotion. This approach has consistently been beneficial for me, and it's something I continuously work on.

THE POWER OF RESILIENCY AND GROWTH

I want to sincerely acknowledge our founder, Bill Elkington, for the crucial and positive decisions he made during a profoundly challenging period, both personally and professionally. Bill is an exceptional individual who I am proud to call my dear friend. He has imparted to me the essence of resilience and growth, evident in those transformative years. Recognizing the need to transition his business, he had to act swiftly due to unforeseen circumstances. Fortunately for our team and me, Bill navigated these decisions in a manner that addressed his personal needs while ensuring the business's integrity and stability. He wisely passed on leadership to those better equipped to manage the situation, given his personal challenges. His journey is a remarkable testament to leadership and resilience, serving as an exemplar for many who might have chosen differently or clung on too long, to their detriment. I am so grateful for Bill for his trust and belief in me as a leader.

HINDSIGHT IS 20/20

Anyone can reflect and recognize things that might have been handled better. I'm no exception. I frequently examine my past as a leader and think, "Oh, I wish I had done certain things differently." What stands out to me, Mike, is that I would've "shot the elephant" sooner. Using the analogy of an elephant in the room, you have to decide if you're going to confront it—and I always say, "Shoot those elephants. Initiate those challenging discussions and make those tough decisions early, because often, situations don't improve." Even though things have progressed since that phase in the business, I sometimes wonder if acting sooner or initiating those tough talks earlier could have expedited the transition and maybe reduced some pain along the way. It's impossible to make the past right, but by reflecting and learning we can make the future better.

Another reflection is that I'd remind my past self that I was put there for a reason. I'm uncertain what led me to that position, but if I was the right fit, then I should fully embrace the role. It's essential to act decisively, spend less time worrying about others' opinions, and more time working with the brilliant people on our team to making impactful decisions, and execute. Surround yourself with individuals who offer valuable advice – not necessarily those you're closest to or even those you like the most, but those who will provide honest feedback, intelligent objective viewpoints and encourage decisiveness.

In retrospect, I'd likely be more proactive and deliberate, rather than spending too much time contemplating my decisions and questioning if I was the right person for the task.

JV DRIVER GROUP

Our business is best described as an investment holding company. Some may refer to it as private equity, a family office, or any other name. In essence, we own other businesses. Our primary sectors include Marine, specifically Heavy Marine. We boast a prominent civil and buildings construction group, an Automotive Group with multiple car dealerships, a Hospitality Group focusing on luxury hotels, and an Insurance Group rooted in London's Lloyd's market. Additionally, we maintain a set of passive investments in our portfolio, where our involvement leans more towards capital provision rather than active business engagement. Geographically, our operations span Canada, the USA, the Caribbean, the United Kingdom, and occasionally Africa, contingent on construction activities with our international team. To provide a scale, we employ between 3,500 and 4,000 individuals, generating over $1 billion in revenue.

The foundation of our businesses is exceptional leadership. At the holding company level, we are a lean team of 8-10; we don't have an everyday operational role with our subsidiary businesses. Our mission has been to establish and back robust, self-reliant teams, each headed by a CEO or President. Our strategy emphasizes granting them autonomy, recognizing their on-ground expertise and capabilities. While we furnish them with capital, it's not merely financial. True, money is abundant, but offering only that would place us in a fiercely competitive commoditized arena. Hence, we supplement financial aid with other resources: governance, leadership development, legal and financial services, and insights on mergers and acquisitions, and business know-how. This approach enables them to tap into our group's collective experience and avoid repetitively confronting identical challenges. Our philosophy prioritizes placing these leaders at the forefront, allowing them autonomy while maintaining a structured governance model featuring deeply engaged board members.

THE IMPORTANCE OF GOOD CORPORATE GOVERNANCE

Governance acts as the speed limit on the highway of autonomy. From an operator's standpoint, governance provides the framework that facilitates the exchange of information and ideas, as well as a consistent rhythm of check-ins to assess the business against its plans making course correction as required. This framework helps ascertain whether the business is on track, quickly spotlighting areas ripe for enhancement or showing promising returns. It also highlights where more effort is needed to meet our plans and strategic growth objectives. When functioning optimally, it not only measures financial outcomes but also forecasts potential risks that could either positively or negatively impact the business.

While governance can sometimes seem impersonal and rigid, when applied effectively, it essentially serves as a structure for leadership. When functioning well, this structure ensures everyone is in alignment, connecting vision with execution by regularly evaluating the business, sharing insights, and aiming for growth. We consider it a vital component in our operations and central to our business management strategy. We firmly believe in the principle of "Good governance, practically implemented." It's not about having meetings for their own sake; it's about meaningful meetings. The objective is to do just enough to pinpoint and cultivate value—be it in terms of satisfaction, financial returns, or any other metric. Value is omnipresent, and the tool to rally everyone around this concept, be it through formal or informal channels, is governance.

MOTIVATORS AND SUCCESS FACTORS

I'm a huge admirer of Winston Churchill. Anything related to Churchill resonates deeply with me, as I think he's possibly the most exceptional leader I've ever studied. He once said, "Success is not final. Failure is not fatal. It is the courage to continue that counts." I think about this quote often, especially when I reflect on Churchill in 1941. With an imperfect track record as a military and political leader he was reluctantly given the premiership when no other candidate came forward. He faced a significant setback at Dunkirk shortly after assuming the role of Prime Minister and effectively became the leader in the European front against the Nazis. Considering the challenges and imperfections he grappled with, his ability to rise to the occasion is truly inspiring. He eventually changed the world through his leadership in rallying nations to fight and win against the evil of the Nazi's. While I don't draw direct parallels between his experiences and mine, I often look at his leadership and think, "How do I define success? What is my purpose? How will I elevate my leadership in the time I have?"

I find immense value in seeking inspiration from the exemplary lives of others, using their legacies to drive impact and add value to our company and team. I'm grateful that our success isn't solely about me. Far from it. It revolves around the incredible individuals who operate our businesses daily and fuel their growth. My role is to integrate my skills into this team, striving for alignment among all its components, aiming to realize our collective objectives. I'm invigorated by this responsibility, always aiming to mirror the qualities of great leaders before me and hoping to make a meaningful contribution in my own right.

SUCCESSION PLANNING AND BUSINESS CONTINUITY

Our approach to succession isn't flawless, and it's an ongoing point of discussion and challenge in various sectors of our company. Though we're not perfect, we're committed to it and aim to continually cultivate strong leaders to take the reins from our current team.

The significance of succession planning can't be overstated. If growth is the objective, it necessitates change, fresh perspectives, capable individuals, a committed workforce, and competent leadership. These elements are essential for scaling up. Often in private businesses, founders or long-standing leaders might operate based more on their personal styles rather than established structures or governance. This mindset can hinder succession planning, as there might be an underlying belief that no one else could match the proficiency of the current leader or that such a leader would be challenging to replace.

To address this, it's crucial to dismantle these notions and contemplate the next steps if the current leader were absent. It's essential to assess if the potential successor exists within the company or if an external search is necessary, and then to take action based on these findings. Though discussing the inevitability of leadership transition can be uncomfortable, astute leaders are always scouting for their successors, as this forward-thinking strategy also paves their path for further contributions. When approached constructively, succession discussions can rejuvenate an organization. We're still refining our strategy in this area, but I firmly believe it's not just crucial for ensuring continuity but also for facilitating growth in the broader business.

GREAT LEADERS EVOLVE

It's my opinion that all leaders are born, great leaders are built. Everyone is born a leader of themselves but by effort, training and a focused commitment to development great leadership can be developed. I don't think you should ever stop learning in whatever trade that you're in. And if your trade is leadership, it's incumbent on people who want to call themselves leaders to strive to be the greatest they can. There's only one way to do that—that's through learning, self-reflection, and taking a very critical look at their own performance with an eye to improve.

My commitment is that I'm on a journey to become a great leader. I don't know when that journey will end. Someday when I'm dead, people will hopefully say, "Hey, that Chuck guy was really good at leadership. Glad he was around." But until then, that story's never written, and it's only going to be likely as good as the trust that I build with people and the ability for me to align everybody around a common goal and to move forward as *part* of the team, not the ego-driven leader of the team. My goal is to lead with minimal ego, continually learn, and consistently strive to offer value in my leadership role.

THE DISCIPLINED AND HOLISTIC LEADER

Looking back, I've reflected a lot on the concept of work-life balance over the years. I've increasingly questioned this idea of work-life balance. My personal belief—which isn't a unique revelation, as many share this view—is that the idea of work-life balance is a myth. The notion of separating work and personal life as distinct entities is misleading; it's *all* life. It's a fallacy to claim, "This is my work, and that's my personal life. I eagerly await my workday's end," or, "I look forward to work because I dislike my personal life." Such comments seem thoughtless. In reality, life is a continuous spectrum. There isn't a demarcation where work ends and personal life begins; nature and the universe certainly don't recognize such distinctions.

I've learned the importance of recognizing what truly brings me satisfaction and understanding my purpose. This involves maintaining physical fitness, striving to improve by 1% every day in areas that matter, and achieving personal goals. This could relate to leadership roles, going to the gym, bodybuilding, or being a devoted parent, spouse, or team leader. Every leadership position, be it leading oneself, others, a team, a family, or an entire organization, demands continuous growth and alignment with one's core values. For me, these values revolve around satisfaction, creating value, and positively impacting those in my circle.

Ultimately, I aspire to contribute in ways that benefit others. I feel a deep-seated urge to utilize whatever skills I possess to add value to others' lives. To do so, I need to be at my best, constantly refining and enhancing my capabilities across various domains. I view this as a personal commitment, a choice that I embrace wholeheartedly.

ENTREPRENEURIAL LEADERSHIP INSIGHTS

I'm a biker, I love motorcycles, and I have lots of tattoos. One of my favourites is a little phrase that says, "Ego is the enemy." I have it positioned where I can always see it. It's always visible when I wear a short-sleeved shirt, which is essential to me. I believe that in many crisis moments, ego comes into play. Whether it's good or bad in business or life in general, I think that a significant challenge to overcome is thinking, "Why me? Why am I here? Why is this happening to me?"

To me, that's just a manifestation of ego. What it conveys is, "I'm too good for this. Why must I deal with this mess? Why does this always happen to me? I'm too significant."

On my best days, I strive to avoid all of those sentiments because they are counterproductive. Instead, one might consider saying, "Why not me? I'm glad this is happening to me because I have the skills and the ability to address this. Maybe I've faced it before, and yes, it's tedious, but we can navigate through it faster this time due to our prior experience." I believe these viewpoints assist people in steering clear of pitfalls without getting trapped in negativity. Keep progressing, and rather than claiming, "I'm too good for this" and allowing ego to dominate—which can become self-destructive—set aside such thoughts, address the situation, and move forward.

From my perspective on life and particularly in business, facing a crisis is not unusual. We all manage risks daily, whether they relate to physical safety, finances, weather, or geopolitical factors, in our personal or professional lives. A crisis is merely another manifestation of change. One can either panic and exclaim, "Oh, why me? This is so challenging. I'm at a loss," or take a proactive stance: "We're going to address this. It's manageable. We'll confront the situation head-on, devise a strategy, and do our utmost to navigate through it, benefiting all involved." To me, this approach embodies leadership. Recognizing that a crisis or significant change is a routine aspect of business is vital.

It's naive to assume otherwise. More often than not, such situations are the norm rather than the exception.

I think that leaders in general need to park their ego and accept the reality that change is constant. If you're going to grow, challenges and change are going to come up. So own it. Choose to be responsible for it, lead yourself and your team, take action and move on.

THE ROAD AHEAD

I am very optimistic about the future. I believe optimism is a choice, and considering all the alternatives, why not choose it? Such a perspective leads to numerous positive outcomes and value. My vision for the future and my perspective is rooted in the belief that the "only thing new in the world is the history we have all forgotten." Many challenges we face today, whether they concern individuals or businesses, echo patterns from the past. While circumstances may differ, we can take solace in the fact that human beings, especially leaders, have confronted similar, if not more daunting, challenges before. Generation after generation, the world has persevered, and everything has generally turned out fine.

When I look at what's to come, I believe we have so much to be thankful for, especially if we emphasize positivity and aim to improve by 1% every day. Strive to be better, to learn more, and to be the best leader you can be, whether it's leading yourself, your team, your business, or your family. The future is rapidly evolving, with the pace of change accelerating and disruptive shifts becoming commonplace. I encourage everyone to view situations with flexibility and a fresh perspective. Given the technological advancements and lessons from the past, we possess a tremendous opportunity to redefine how businesses function and interact with their stakeholders in the future.

I think that, under the best circumstances, we'll find ourselves in a virtual, flexible, career-oriented environment that allows people to contribute to the maximum extent of their abilities, aligned with an overall vision and plan within a business or any organization they find themselves in. It's my belief that the emerging focus on leadership from various sources offers anyone an incredible opportunity to accelerate their growth. Unlike 2,000 years ago, when you might have had to attend lectures of a stoic in person and, if fortunate enough, obtain some form of media like a scroll for portability of knowledge, today we have access to a wealth of information right at our fingertips. It's affordable and easily accessible. I believe that if we harness this knowledge to our advantage, we'll achieve excellent outcomes in business, entrepreneurship, and beyond.

I'd say: cast aside fear, focus on the positives, and explore the possibilities to create value wherever you are. We're either entering or already living in an exceptional era. While it's not without challenges, every challenge presents an opportunity. We all have the capacity to take initiative and lead in various capacities, capitalizing on these chances and achieving the satisfaction we all seek.

A COMMENT FROM MIKE

Chuck, that is why a great leader like you is in this book, and I can say for the record that we've enjoyed lunch together a few times, which is great.

A few things really resonate with me as we close out, are your comments about optimism being a choice. Years back, I wrote a blog titled "The Optimist, the Pessimist, and the Realist." My perspective has shifted quite a bit since then. I am an optimist by design and nature, but I'm also a realist. I've set aside the pessimistic viewpoint because, being realistic, I know I'm not going to achieve everything I desire in life. However, by making an effort to move in the right direction, I'm bound to attain something more, different, or better compared to the pessimist, who remains skeptical about everything and does nothing but challenge the beliefs of others.

Your earlier comment about challenges resonates with me, along with "success leaves clues. Missed opportunities and challenges also leave numerous clues." There are many lessons to be gleaned from challenges, whether in our personal or professional lives. As you mentioned earlier, Chuck, some of the leadership lessons you've learned involved recognizing what not to do. Leveraging these insights is a golden opportunity. If you read enough books, you'll become wiser. Applying the knowledge you gain from such books further cultivates that wisdom. Chuck, I hold you in high regard as a leader, and it's an honor to know you professionally. I'm also privileged to play a role in supporting some of the leaders within JV Driver Group.

CLOSING COMMENTS FROM CHUCK

Mike, I really agree with the statements you just made, I align with them. One of the greatest sources of inspiration for me is the ancient philosophy of stoicism. I derive much from it. I value the four core virtues and they represented in a tattoo on my right arm. I see them always and do my best to live to them. I believe there is abundant wisdom therein that's directly applicable to leaders, especially those in business. It fundamentally comes down to the truth of understanding what is in your control, personal responsibility, personal choices, and doing what is necessary with humility and without ego to move your team forward. Whether you lead a team of one or a team of thousands, all these principles still apply. If you can improve by 1% every day, as I often say, you will find yourself constantly bettering not only yourself but also those around you. I encourage anyone who reads your book or hears these words to persevere. Focus on self-improvement and reflect on your journey over time. As I mentioned earlier, the only new thing in the world is the history we've all forgotten. Many have walked before us, and many were exceptional.

As the President & CEO of JV Driver Group, Chuck Sanders is responsible for the Company's worldwide portfolio and operations, including opportunity acquisition, governance & execution. He also leads corporate planning and is responsible for the implementation of the group's strategic plan and investment activity.

Prior to his current role, Chuck was the Company's CFO. Chuck is an experienced senior executive and has extensive business and financial experience across a diversity of industries as an investor, advisor, and operator. Chuck is a Certified Corporate Director, Certified Public Accountant and holds a Bachelor of Commerce degree. Chuck has also completed extensive corporate finance training from Wharton Business School.

3

It's Not About Me

Mary Cameron and
Corporate Service

ARY CAMERON'S JOURNEY FROM GRAPPLING
with academic challenges to academic excellence
taught her that true wealth lies not in status or
financial gain, but in the values one embraces. She navigated
the realms of life and business with aplomb, emerging as a val-
ue-driven leader with a tangible impact. Her extensive executive
experience spans across real estate, insurance, IT, and utilities.
Beyond her CEO role, she's served as Deputy Minister in two
provinces. Mary is a Principal with Ozone Advisory Group and is
a full-time Director and Chair.

In the fall of 2021, she was elected as the incoming chair of
Habitat for Humanity International's board of directors. She is
the first Canadian and first non-U.S. citizen to hold the position.

I have known of Mary for many years, but only started focusing on building a great professional relationship with her in 2019, through a Corporate Governance program that I was enrolled in at the University of Alberta. Since then, we have spent meaningful time connecting, including my involvement in Private Company Governance Program that her business Ozone Advisory leads; "Just for Chairs". Her business helps transform your perceptions of governance and discover the path to high-performing boards. It is facilitated by C-Suite industry leaders with decades of experience as directors and chairs, this comprehensive program combines governance theory with real-world practical experience.

I am most grateful for Mary's meaningful contribution to my book.

GROWING UP

As a child I lived in my own little world. In grade one, everyone else had a school uniform. I never even noticed we had school uniforms. My mother saw it on the pictures, and she said, "My goodness, didn't you notice that everyone else was dressed differently?" I didn't know how to read until grade two the teachers thought I should be held back because I was slow. My mother is the one who eventually taught me to read because she realized I had memorized all the books and that I was just pretending to read.

I hated school and being in public. I just wanted to live in my own little world. Until one day I realized the people who got good marks, the teacher left alone. So, I thought, "Aha. I better get good marks. That's my way of avoiding attention." I also was horribly shy, so I hated being called on, then I noticed all the pupils who raised their hands never got called on. I started getting excellent marks and raising my hand all the time...all to avoid attention. I went from being someone they thought was slow to, in grade six, to one being grouped among the 'students that got good marks. They separated the "smarties" and of course everyone hated us because we were special. We all banded together and decided to infiltrate the yearbook, newspaper and cheerleading team so the kids wouldn't isolate us.

LEARNING TO NAVIGATE THE WORLD

Those tough school days taught me how to get what I want in life, which turned out to be key to my success. My mom didn't have much money, but she gave us something better: a passion for doing things well and caring for others. She showed us how to live richly without a lot of cash.

This upbringing taught me that money and status aren't everything; it's the values that count. Heading into college, I was all about science and thought about becoming a doctor. That is until our family doctor warned me off, painting a grim picture of the profession. Looking back, I see he was just bitter, but his words steered me away from medical school.

I ended up with a degree in zoology/ecology and landed a government job, which was a far cry from what I'd studied. But life took another turn when a private developer spotted me negotiating and offered me a job. I jumped from government work to the private sector, and from there, into engineering and technology. I just followed the opportunities, which is how I got the reputation of being someone who adapts and thrives on change. Over time, I learned that I didn't need to know everything about a job to succeed. I just needed to gather a great team, manage them well, and support them in reaching our goals.

THE MILITARY'S ROLE IN MY JOURNEY

My dad was an Army major, and because he was often away and then my parents divorced, I didn't get to know him well. My memories of Army life and moving around places like Belleville and Shiloh aren't fond, and I grew up with a bit of a bias against the military culture. This even affected my hiring decisions, steering me away from applicants with a military background. But that changed when my friend Doug Cox called me. He was involved with the Loyal Edmonton Regiment and asked if I knew any women who might want to join as an honorary member.

After learning more about the role, I realized my bias was holding me back. So, I decided to dive in and accepted the position of honorary lieutenant-colonel. The military struggles to recruit and retain women, and I see that their deep-rooted cultures and traditions need to evolve. I believe I can be a connector between the military and our community. By being involved as a woman, I hope to start conversations, change perspectives, and serve as a role model for women's roles in the military.

WHAT IS AN HONORARY LIEUTENANT-COLONEL?

The goal is to have honoraries act as links between the community and the military, helping people see military service as a valuable part of career development, especially for its leadership and diverse training opportunities.

We're working to get Edmonton to understand and appreciate the military's aims. I'm now advising my peers to consider military backgrounds, like those of reservists, as a plus on resumes because of the leadership skills gained.

I've always given extra credit to Saskatchewan farmers on a resume, valuing their self-reliance and industrious nature. The idea is that if you're on your own in the field and run into trouble, you learn to figure things out yourself. It's about being resourceful and knowing that work sometimes comes before the end of the day. I used to look for this self-reliance in potential hires, but I've shifted my focus. The military training these young folks receive is outstanding. They're learning to lead in a very hands-on way, and I'm keen to show others how this is a real asset in the business world.

MY LEADERSHIP PHILOSOPHY

I really believe every person would rather go home at night and say, "I did a great job today," rather than, "I skated by. I scammed the system."

I think people want to do a good job, and if they know what *great* is, they'd rather do a great job than a good job. Our main job as leaders is to make sure everyone knows what a great job looks like. It's not some highbrow concept; it's about being so straightforward that everyone feels they can pitch in. Trust that people naturally want to excel. A top-notch leader offers chances and guidance on how someone can tap into their unique strength, their superpower, if you will.

Everyone is good at something. How can they harness that to help reach our collective goals? The best leader is convinced that everyone has a superpower and provides them the chance to shine at work. When the vision is crystal clear, everyone knows exactly where we're headed. It's as simple as that!

MY LEADERSHIP SUPERPOWER

I think my real superpower is I'm an optimist and I believe in people. I truly believe things can be better.

I also believe in people; I believe everyone has something to contribute. We just need to take the time to listen and really find out what people are good at that's how you become a team player. I'd rather be part of a team than the individual on the stage getting the award; I'd much rather be sharing the accomplishment.

If I boil it down, my superpower is finding what's in a person that can be brought out, and then giving the individual the opportunity to use that ability in the achievement of the goals.

PROUDEST ACHIEVEMENTS

Early in my time with Habitat, I was part of the Edmonton board. Back then, we were proud to build one to three homes a year. At a board retreat, we had a moment of clarity: the few homes we built were life-changing for those families, yet against the backdrop of need, they were just a drop in the ocean. We asked ourselves, "What if we could construct 100 homes every year? And what if, for every home we built locally, we also built one internationally?" We started calling this vision "100, 100 and more"—the 'more' symbolized our ambition to also transform the conversation around housing importance.

That goal reshaped our mindset. Suddenly, Edmonton was leading Canada in Habitat builds for the next decade. We never quite hit the 100 mark, but we consistently increased our build numbers year over year. We started thinking bigger: we revamped our processes, planned our land purchases years in advance, and secured multi-year funding commitments.

I remember speaking on the national board when a fellow director questioned the depth of our new mantra. During a tour of our prefab centre—an innovative concept for Habitat—one of the national board members asked a machine operator why he was there. His reply was pure gold: "I'm cutting this wall, sure, but I'm really here because we're committed to building 100 homes. And with every local home, we'll add one more internationally. We believe in '100, 100, and more,' and we're determined to change how our community thinks about housing." The board member was so taken aback he wondered if the worker was staged. But it was genuine—the belief was universal among us.

By changing the mindset, you don't have to worry about everything else. People will make it happen.

Mary in centre, with Jimmy Carter, 39th President of the United States of America, and her Habitat for Humanity colleagues.

ANOTHER PROUD MOMENT

When I went to WCB Alberta as CEO (Workers Compensation Board), it was a hierarchical culture and most of the executive and management positions were filled by men—really judgmental men, at that. I wanted to unite the organization around creating the atmosphere and processes to get injured workers back to work, but I faced the fundamental challenge that we had two sides to the organization.

- Side #1: We had the employer services side who served all the employers and were often focused predominantly on their rates and their costing.
- Side #2: We had the injured worker services side that made sure injured workers got good medical care and good benefits.

The two sides of the organization had different cultures even different IT systems. And they argued with each other all the time. Neither was primarily focused on return to work.

Dealing with these two discrete sides of the organization was a huge obstacle. To fix the division, we reorganized the entire staff into industry teams. It meant that we physically moved over 600 of our staff. They worked side by side to understand each other's workplace demands and culture. Over time, we developed a closer relationship with employers and workers and could assist the return-to-work process by facilitating the connection between the workers and the employers.

By the time I left, everything had turned around. We had some of the lowest industry attrition rates in Canada, some of the highest benefits, and a high 'fairness' rating from workers and employers.

WORK-LIFE BALANCE SECRETS

Balance isn't something I strive for daily or even weekly, but over time, I stay true to what's important to me. I've learned to delegate relentlessly, outsourcing whatever I can to free up my time. For instance, cleaning my house is something I haven't done in years, not only because I can, but also because it provides employment for someone who values that work. When it comes to to-do lists, I'm quick to strike off the less critical items at the bottom. I'm always on the lookout for the most efficient approach to anything I do.

Perfection isn't my goal—I focus on what's "good enough." If something doesn't need the extra 20% effort for perfection, I won't spend my time on it. Sharing my passions with my family is also crucial for me. Whether it's a build or a business trip, I bring them along so we can create memories together. I couldn't always be there for every school event, so I teamed up with a mother who could, ensuring I stayed in the loop. I believe being a mom and a role model means pushing myself in my career. Making two careers and family life work has been possible thanks to my incredible partner Alan and my resilient kids.

BOARD SERVICE

Judy Costco, a friend and a volunteer and philanthropist, called me one day and asked if I would co-chair the Women Build for Habitat for Humanity Edmonton. (HFHE), which ended up being a huge job since they weren't known in the area and had never had a Women Build. So, with Susan Green as the other co-chair, we recruited a board, equipped them with pink hard hats, and it blossomed from there. Susan, and I along with our 600 volunteers, helped put Habitat on the map here.

When the build was a great success, Habitat asked Susan and me to join the board. After my term was up at Edmonton, they suggested I go on the national board, so I got elected to Habitat for Humanity Canada (HFHC) and became Chair. And six years later I got appointed to the Habitat for Humanity International Board (HFHI).

It was such an honour to be on the board of HFHI with such a phenomenal group of people. When I first joined the international board, there were four women out of 24 members. One of our goals was to improve gender and geographic diversity—and we have definitely accomplished that! I have enjoyed the honour of being Chair of the international board of Habitat for Humanity International.

I realize I've sat on over three dozen boards and about a third of them are not for profit. A third of them are crowns (Government) and a third of them are private or public. When I left WCB, I actually thought I was looking for another CEO job. I got offered a big one in BC. I almost took it, but then I realized I'd be commuting to my family. I had to decline. I was still looking for another CEO role, but then it hit me—I was genuinely enjoying life while serving on five different boards. I asked myself, "Why chase after the non-stop hustle of being a CEO when I'm happy with what I'm doing?" That's when it clicked: I had become a person dedicated to board governance. For the last fifteen years, I've found real joy in this work.

OZONE ADVISORY GROUP

My business partner, Darren Rawson, and I crossed paths at Cougar Drilling, where he was CEO and I was the Chair. After he moved on, we stayed in contact and found we were both often invited to join various boards. We realized we couldn't accept every offer, but we saw an opportunity to help these boards improve. That's how Ozone Advisory Group was born, with a mission to transform adequate boards into high-performing ones.

We delved into what constitutes a great board and understood that a board's true potential is unlocked only with deliberate effort.

Our work has led to the creation and transformation of numerous boards. We identified that the linchpin often was the chairperson's role. To address this, we established 'Just for Chairs'—a peer learning group for chairs to hone their leadership. This initiative has become a goldmine for us in assembling effective boards.

Additionally, we run a course called 'Private Company Governance' to teach the essentials of sound governance to owners, directors, and C-suite executives.

Our enthusiasm grows as we recognize there's always more to learn, and that a well-crafted board can be an organization's secret weapon. Contrary to the common view of boards as a mere checkbox, I've come to champion the profound impact they can have. Having once been a CEO who merely managed my board without harnessing its full value, I now advocate fervently for the power of good governance.

THE BENEFITS OF BOARDS

First, there are two most common types of boards, Advisory or Fiduciary.

An *advisory board* isn't ultimately accountable for the business. Typically, they're hired by the founder or the CEO,

The *fiduciary board* is ultimately accountable for the business, and they hire and fire the CEO. We like to have an advisory board feel like a fiduciary board. So, they should have an agenda. They should ask management to be accountable the two should feel the same. But at the end of the day, the fiduciary board has the final accountability for the business, and typically, the advisory board is hired and fired by the CEO as opposed to the other way around.

Nearly every sizable company, especially those eyeing growth or change, could use a board. A board's real value lies in its ability to critique the strategy and maintain strategic focus. It also introduces a level of accountability and discipline that's tough for any CEO to self-impose. CEOs love the thrill of the new and the next big thing, often at the expense of the disciplined focus on the right performance indicators and strategies essential for driving the business.

The role of a board chair is often misunderstood, thanks to Hollywood's portrayal of them as the ultimate decision-maker. In reality, a board chair needs a high emotional quotient, and surprisingly, deep industry experience isn't always necessary. Sometimes, it's advantageous to bring in someone from a different industry to avoid any knowledge competition with the CEO. What's critical is an understanding of group dynamics, a knack for process, and the ability to listen and ask the right questions.

A chair's relationship with the CEO should be built on mutual respect, with the chair working behind the scenes, focused on enhancing the CEO's ability to execute the company's strategy. This dynamic was clear when I served as the Board Chair for Cougar Drilling. They brought me in not for my expertise in drilling or finance, but for my ability to identify risks and foster key discussions.

Succession planning is often a topic of discussion among leaders, but I prefer to think of it as "human capital development" or "talent management." After all, businesses are fundamentally about people. It's common to hear that people are a company's most important asset, yet there's usually little effort put into managing this asset. Discussions should revolve around the company's culture, required skillsets, and leadership styles. Before I left WCB, I had prepared three VPs for the top job, each a fit for different future scenarios of the company.

Boards need to be future-oriented, always asking "what if?" about scenarios like a CEO's sudden departure or a shift in business. It's not just about one contingency plan but exploring all possibilities and preparing even for the unexpected. In my view, at least one board meeting a year should be dedicated to discussing talent—where it's thriving, where it's lacking, and how to bridge those gaps.

HOW GREAT LEADERS STAND OUT

Mackenzie Scott is someone I deeply admire for her deliberate efforts in donating a significant portion of her wealth to community causes that make a real impact. Her approach is extraordinary.

Instead of simply handing out cheques for applause, she's taken a more thoughtful route. She enlisted a firm to rigorously find the most deserving recipients, insisting on staying anonymous throughout to keep the focus off herself and firmly on the cause. Her commitment goes beyond the spotlight; it's about effecting genuine change, including substantial support for Habitat for Humanity Internationally.

Earlier in the year, our CEO Jonathan Reckford hinted at a major anonymous donation. I immediately guessed Mackenzie Scott. I had been following her philanthropic journey, and her style of making a difference lined up. Sure enough, her meticulous due diligence had been at play. She funneled donations directly to our affiliates, leading to moments of disbelief among the recipients. Calls were made to affiliates, informing them of multi-million-dollar donations, which they initially mistook for pranks. But it was all true—no phishing, just pure philanthropy.

Suddenly, out of nowhere, she directed substantial gifts to chosen affiliates. For Habitat, this meant a staggering $436 million, with $20 million allocated to our international office. The best part? The funds come without restrictions. She asks for nothing more than an annual update over three years to share the impact her gift has made. No strings attached.

CLARITY OF INTENTION

Great leaders have a knack for keeping the big picture in focus. It starts with clarity - if you say, "We want to build a house," that's a start. But then you add, "on the hill, with a green roof and four pillars," and it becomes a vision that others can start to believe in, too. "With a back door made of steel," and suddenly, the image is so clear that everyone can see it, believe in it, and work towards it. The best leaders constantly remind their teams of this vivid picture, detailing what the world will look like when their goals are reached.

Take Zelensky, the President of Ukraine, as an example. Each time he speaks, he's crystal clear about his country's needs. He consistently calls for help, radiating a belief in success and the conviction that the cause is worth any cost. He's intentional in his leadership, always reinforcing what he needs and where they're headed.

Above all, the finest leaders deeply understand that achievements are the sum of people's individual efforts. They value every single contribution because they know that's the true foundation of any success.

PERSONAL AND PROFESSIONAL BUCKET LIST

One of my bucket list goals is to expand the quality and reach of Ozone Group's offerings. I've also got my heart set on extended family trips. Last January, we had a blast at Milligan Manor in Jasper, Alberta, a place with eight bedrooms for all the kids and grandkids. It was such a hit that we've decided to make it an annual thing. This year, it's Mexico. With five children, nine grandchildren, and the tenth on the way, it was special to see the cousins and siblings creating shared memories.

I'm determined to continue making a mark with Ozone, especially in governance. I'm also committed to the companies I work with and the journeys I'm on with them. No plans to step down anytime soon—I'm always on the lookout for new opportunities. Predicting the future isn't my strong suit, but I'm open to whatever may come.

Lately, I've zeroed in on four core values that guide me, especially when setting up boards or choosing directors. Curiosity is one – I'm always astounded by how much there is to learn. Then there's wisdom, which for me is about learning from experiences, not just having them. Courage is essential, too; it's about making the tough but right choices, despite fear. And humility – knowing I'm far from perfect gives others space to shine.

On days when things don't go right, reflecting on these values—wisdom, curiosity, courage, and humility—usually shows me what was lacking. Staying true to these principles is what I strive for, to make both the good days and the challenging ones better.

DEFINITION OF SUCCESS

I think success is living my values.

If I can do that over time, that's a successful life. I love big goals. I'm competitive. I love achieving things. I love achieving tough things. But again, not by myself. The fun and joy of being with a team and collectively accomplishing something is amazing. I love having an impact. I love working with other people.

Success looks like working with other people in a joyous way, in a way that takes an awful lot of energy to achieve something important. That's success.

Everyone operates on a set of values, whether they realize it or not. These values are the filters through which we make our decisions. For instance, if you consistently prioritize profit in your decision-making, it becomes clear that profitability is a core value for you. On the other hand, if kindness guides your choices, then kindness is one of your fundamental values. Most people haven't taken the time to formally identify and define their values, but they are there, silently shaping every choice.

It's worthwhile for everyone to reflect and ask themselves: *what are my values?*

FINAL THOUGHTS

The best company for an afternoon's conversation doesn't always come from those who loom largest in life. I enjoy the company of folks who might not be celebrated by society but who are genuine, kind, fascinating, and impactful. Being open to learning about others has become even more important to me during this post-COVID time, reinforcing that we're not made for isolation. It's the people who build bridges, who really listen and care, that make a difference. When I talk to someone, I aim to be as authentic as I can, going beyond surface-level interactions. Even through a Zoom screen, I'm not afraid to share a part of myself. It's not our achievements but our true selves that matter most at the end of the day.

Mary Cameron, ICD.D is a Principal at Ozone Advisory Group Inc. Mary is a former CEO and executive with experience in real estate, insurance, IT, and utilities. She was also a former Deputy Minister in two provinces. Mary is a full-time Director and Chair and has made a long-term commitment to Habitat for Humanity currently serving as Chair of Habitat for Humanity International.

4

People First

Bruce Kirkland and Lexus of Edmonton

HEN IT COMES TO IMPRESSIVE EDMONTON leaders, Bruce Kirkland is on the list. He has incredible business savvy, but his people skills and passion to make a difference with people and organizations is truly incredible. He gives back to the community and sponsors more charities and events than I can count.

Bruce was born in McLennan, Alberta and he started day one at Lexus of Edmonton in 2004 when the dealership first opened. His first role was the General Manager and he evolved to Dealer Principal. Now he's President and CEO. He is a lifelong learner and has shared many must reads with me over the years. *The*

Go-Giver, Everything Counts, and *The 10 Golden Rules of Customer Service: The Story of the $6,000 Egg* are some of my favourites.

I've been privileged to know Bruce since late 2010 through our connection with Synergy Network, a group of 100+ business leaders and owners—both Bruce and I served as Board Chair to the organization years ago. Bruce has become a dear friend and a man I hold in high regard.

THE EARLY YEARS OF A LEADER'S JOURNEY

One thing most people probably don't know about me: I come from a family of eleven. There are eight boys and three girls. I say I'm number seven, lucky seven. Seven of eleven. I think a lot of my DNA, or what I believe in, came from watching my mom and my dad raise up just shy of a dozen kids. During that time, we had just moved from Edmonton. Growing up, my parents were my examples of hard work and giving back.

I have always wanted to be involved in some type of leadership role. After I began with Synergy Network it was not long before I was social director for Synergy, which would eventually lead me to the role of president. But my ambition started before then.

Getting involved in the community and leadership started early. In high school, I had to be on the student council. In university, I had to be president of my class. When I worked in the Sherbrooke community, I had to be the sports director of the community league.

My entrepreneurial background values education first, but I'm not above following a good opportunity. My friend came to me with a great opportunity to start a business. I was ready for a change so jumped in. Off I went and he took care of the technical side of the business. He was an expert at property tax evaluations for the government, but he had limited people skills, so I was to be the sales guy. I became the face of the company.

So, I took a year off from education and was knocking on doors and making cold calls. That's when I started my networking journey. I thought, if I'm going to build a business, how am I going to build it? I'm not going to open the door and they're just going to come; I needed to network and meet people. I knew that this was the key to success.

We started our property tax company and over the years it boomed, and we did very, very well. When you do very well and you're a small company, someone comes and knocks on your door, right? Deloitte bought us so they could start a national property tax division.

I worked in Edmonton and travelled to Toronto and Vancouver to build the national practice by signing big national contracts for them. Businesses like Home Depot, Oxford, and Earls wanted to have their properties looked at. I lasted there probably two years.

We did great, everyone was happy, and they were impressed with my drive and professionalism. They also told me I was working too hard. In the end, the culture was not a fit for me.

BUILD IT, GET BOUGHT OUT, BUILD SOMETHING ELSE

Then my old business partner, who had left when we got bought, contacted me, "Let's start an offsite document storage company."

"What's offsite document storage?" I said, "I know nothing about it."

He goes, "Again, Bruce, it's about people. Don't worry about it. You're great with people and there is a big opportunity here." So, I jumped to a new challenge.

My three new partners then said to me, "You have no money, but you know everybody in Edmonton, go buy us a building so we can get started."

I went out, found the building, and they bought the building. It's an old beautiful MacCosham dock building behind Grant MacEwan University in Edmonton. It's still there!

Now, they said to me, "You have no money, but you can buy into the real estate in the first five years at the cost of this today." I built the business, and they didn't do much.

THE IMPORTANCE OF MENTORSHIP

My mentor, Herb Anton, who was the original founder of Toyota/Lexus, told me you should be a lifelong learner and you should find a mentor, especially if you're going to be an entrepreneur. Herb always gave me great advice, so I chose him to guide me. I think people forget about the importance of finding a mentor.

Herb and I would meet, and I always complained that I didn't have very good partners. Herb said, "Bruce, I watched you build your business with Deloitte across Canada and now this company. You're in another partnership you don't like. Let's test them. Test them, Bruce."

I go, "What do you mean, test them?"

He clarified, "Go and tell them you have the money to buy into the real estate side."

"I don't have the money," I protested.

"No, no, we'll get the money," he reassured me. That's when he taught me about leveraging the bank. "The bank has the money. It's real estate, Bruce."

So, I went to my partners and declared, "I'm buying in, I have the money."

They said, "Oh, no, no, that agreement changed."

I said, "What do you mean that's changed?"

"No, no."

Sadly, it was all verbal. There was no written contract, and of course, the offer tested their integrity. It didn't mean I'd get something out of it.

I went back to Herb. "They're not going to let me buy in."

He goes, "I knew it." At that point in time, he had the Kingsway Lexus dealership and he said to me, "Well, look, Lexus wants me to build a free-standing store. Why don't you go do that for me? And just keep working there." I agreed to find the property for him.

I found him several options, but he turned it back to me. "Which one do you want?" "Which one do I want? It's your business. I don't care," I replied.

Herb insisted, "Tell me what you think is the best property, Bruce."

"170th Street in Edmonton, Herb."

"Okay. So go buy it."

Off I went and bought it. I was learning a lot during that time. After the property closed, Herb announced, "Well, you're going to be my General Manager."

I looked at him incredulously, "What? Of the Lexus store? Herb, I don't know anything about the auto industry. I don't know anything about cars."

He took his glasses off and looked intently at me, "Young man, it's not about cars, is it? It's about people. I've watched you for almost fifteen years, Bruce. You got a gift with people. You can do this, you already built two other companies!"

We talked about it for two weeks before I decided to take the plunge and do it. It was a great challenge, but I built the store, and the rest is history.

One of the problems with entrepreneurs is they think they know it all. Or they're afraid to surround themselves with people stronger than them. Without having a mentor to help having guide you, to help you grow, I wouldn't have been here.

RULES TO LIVE BY AND GROW YOUR BUSINESS

Aside from finding a good mentor, I've found there's a short list of other rules to live by when you want to grow a business.

- Value your customers.
- Always surround yourself with people stronger than you.
- Empower the people around you—do not micromanage.
- Always express your gratitude to your team and spend money on training them.
- If you empower and engage the people around you, you're going to look great.
- Many entrepreneurs are afraid someone's going to be better than them, don't fall for that.
- Do not be afraid to do it.
- Set goals, review them, strive for them, and set high expectations.
- Prioritize your time and stick to it. Make as much time for yourself, as you do others.
- Twelve-hour days won't make you as successful as a balanced, happy life will.
- Network.
- Planning is key. It is great to dream but you need to plan!
- Make sure you have a great accountant and lawyer.
- Support the community that you live in.

EMPOWERING YOUR TEAM FOR THE JOURNEY

Out of all these rules, I want to emphasize empowering your team for the journey ahead. You must empower your team. You must believe in them. Mentor them. Bring them with you along the way.

Don't hide things from them. If you're struggling, say, "Hey, we're struggling here. Do you have an idea? What do you think? How can we improve this?" Your team may have great ideas and feel empowered if you listen to them.

As leaders, we don't have to have all the answers. I try hard not to get into the weeds, but it happens. Your people can be an asset to you. Coaches, mentors, your employees—all have different points of view. Everyone brings a new pair of glasses to the scene. A whole new set of eyes can see your business through a new lens. If you are lost in the weeds, ask someone to give you the helicopter view—they can see things you can't. The more eyes the better!

Even people outside your company will help you. I use people outside my industry all the time to get different ideas. I don't go to auto conferences. They don't do anything for me. Because when you think about it, if you are all in the same neighborhood and no one ever leaves the neighborhood, there will never be any new information or ideas coming in. Don't get me wrong, I go to lots of conferences. I'm a big believer in Disney conferences. But the auto conferences don't do much for me. It's all the same stuff.

I encourage business owners to look outside their industry when looking for mentors or professional help. Their strengths may help you. When I opened the dealership, I had a whole new set of eyes because I wasn't from the industry. That was a huge part of our success. I always asked the Why question and challenged old processes.

In sum, don't be afraid to ask for help. Successful CEOs are people with mentors and teams that aren't afraid to bring people on the train.

A DIFFERENT VIEW ON HIRING

I had the dealership's building built, I had an ad out, and I was starting to hire staff. I was really excited because that was a brand-new opportunity. One day, I interviewed a pile of people, all from auto industry. At that end of that day, I didn't know what I was going to do.

They'd said, "I've sold more metal. I'm top of the board." That's all I heard about. "Oh, I out gross all my teammates." "I am the best salesman." I sensed a trend.

I'm sitting there going, this is what this business is. This is what I asked one gentleman. I said, "You sell ten, fifteen cars a month. Can you give me some references, two clients or two guests you sold to, that I can call and will give you a reference?"

Flustered, he responded, "Why would you want to do that? Why would you want to call one of my clients?"

I struggled with that mentality. That's when a light went on in my head. Why don't I hire people out of hospitality or a different industry? People who knew people? I went back, threw all the car resumes out, and went to the people with no experience in the auto industry but tons with customer service. I hired all of them.

We can always train people on the technical side, but the key is the social side, the relationship side. People come first.

PUTTING PEOPLE FIRST

You know the great thing about hiring people outside of the auto industry? They don't have any baggage. I went to hospitality because, as I've said, it's all about people and they have great people skills. It's been unbelievable.

Many times, when people are hiring, they are afraid to go outside the box. They think you need somebody who knows their particular business. But the truth is, you really don't. In fact, it may be better.

The key is to spend money and train your teams. People can learn new skills, but only if you invest in them, only if you spend time training them, and only if you empower them. If you invest in them, and they'll invest in you.

Smart leaders put people first. People often ask if leadership is something that people are born with, or can it be learned? One of my mentors doesn't believe in customer first. He believes in employees first. If your employees are happy at their job, they do a good job. When they are doing a good job, the customers feel good. I took this to heart and applied it to my leadership style.

But if you don't invest in your employees to train them, how are they going to be successful? How are they going to be happy if you don't empower them? If you micromanage them?

Not only are your customers happy when your employees are happy, but you have less turnover as well. Investing in our employees has been a key to our success.

LEADERS DON'T NEED A TITLE

I love Robin Sharma. He has a book that everybody that comes onto my management team receives and needs to read. It's called *The Leader with No Title*. You do not have to have a title to lead. Leadership's not about having a title. Leadership's not about how long you've been in a company. You don't have to work five years to be a leader in my store. You can lead without a title. I want you to be a leader out of the gate.

You need to tell people, "Just because I have a title it doesn't mean that I'm a leader." That idea can flip, "Just because I'm a leader, it doesn't mean I have a title."

We do a couple of things at my business that I think people should do. I do a thing called opportunities and challenges. Every manager gets the document. They have to meet with their department, and they go through the challenges and the opportunities. They do it with their department so they can create it together. It helps us get their department's vision and plan for the following year.

Then we put it together. We go offsite and look at each department's presentation. The greatest thing is that another department can help you with a challenge. Maybe another department could offer the opportunity. That's the best thing about engaging the whole team and not putting everyone in silos. I'll admit, the best ideas have not come from me. They don't even always come from the department managers. No, the best ideas have come from the bottom up, our detailers or concierge team. They have a different set of glasses.

If you hire someone, let them contribute. Otherwise, why did you hire them? They don't need a title to lead, and any leader can help your business be successful. By allowing them to be leaders, you also get employees engaged by making them feel like a valued member of the team. They know they're important, and they feel they are making an impact. As leaders, we respect each other. We have high expectations. We embrace change.

To be good leaders, we need to admit we don't know it all. We need to ask other members of our team—VPs down to EAs, receptionists, and detailers. Some of our top ideas have come from our staff, and those ideas come from empowering people to contribute.

CULTURE TRAINING

I wanted to do it all. I think all entrepreneurs want to do it all. But a successful entrepreneur realizes they can't do it all and surrounds themselves with good people. Once you have those people, listen to them—really listen!

Hire slow and fire fast. I truly believe that. If we've got some-one that's struggling and we let them go, I always call them in and ask, "What did we do wrong? What did we miss here? What did we miss in the onboarding? Did we not train them enough? Did we miss that they weren't strong enough? Did we fail or did they fail?"

I believe in my heart that if we hire somebody, invest in them, and they fail, we have some of that ownership. Many companies say, "Oh, we should have never hired them. They were awful." But to me it goes both ways, and if your employees are failing, you better look at your process and see if it includes everyone. For us, *everyone* has to go through culture training. It's not just the management team or the sales team. The detailers, the technicians, the service writers, everybody must come to the training, because they are all part of the team.

When new employees start, I joke, "You came to the auto industry, didn't think you were going to have to read a book and do homework!" But that's part of our culture training, reading a book called *The 10 Golden Rules of Customer Service: The Story of the $6,000 Egg.*

What's it about? How one egg cost a company $6,000!

The egg represents the costly mistake of taking away customer satisfaction from profitability. Even little decisions or talks can create customers for life. The little things can make such a big difference for success. It's a great little picture book.

During culture training, everybody in there must contribute by answering the following: How can we improve the store? What ideas do you have for the store? What can we do better for you? The great thing about culture training is after every session we always have great ideas that wouldn't exist if the training didn't include people from all departments—we would miss out.

I believe all entrepreneurs need to do culture training with their employees even if the employees have been there seven years. It's a time to refresh and create new ideas together. Especially if they've been there seven years, they've seen lots of things you do wrong, and they have ideas to fix them, which will continue to improve your DNA.

WHY PEOPLE LEAVE

If employees are quitting, you have to be proactive. Sit with your employees, either one-on-one or in small groups. Take ownership of whether they go or stay.

During the Great Resignation, many businesses made the mistake of believing people left because of money. We pay well here. We have great benefits. Everybody should have that because you should care for your people, always. But sometimes you only care for your people if they're helping you and your business.

People leave for a variety of reasons, it's your job to learn why. You must take the time to figure it out, and that starts with getting to know your staff. What do you know about your employee outside the business? Do you know their name? Their family members names? Do you know how many kids they have? Do you know if they travel? What do you really know about them?

Here's a great example of what you can learn by reaching out. The other day I was speaking to a lady we have in our Parts Dept. She was in another company for four years. I go down and see her. She had only been with us a short time and was shocked when I called her by name and asked how she was doing. She said, "I can't believe you know my name."

I replied, "What do you mean? You work here."

She sniffed, "I worked at a place where the owner never said hello to me. He didn't even know my name."

I couldn't resist the follow up, "Well, how's your daughter that lives in LA doing now?" She was shocked.

Paying attention to people's interests and strengths isn't just for the people under you. Those same relationship tools work to show care for people over you. Herb, our late founder, was probably thinking about me as part of his succession plan long before I was aware I was next in line. Remember, Herb and I had been friends for twenty-five years before I ever went to work for him. He was a very quiet man, very humble and kind. People would say, "How can you spend time with Herb? He doesn't even talk." I go, "Because you don't listen to him. He's a great storyteller if you just listen."

When I started bringing Herb out, he was very shy. I'd bring him to events here at the store and when I'd introduce him, I'd say, "Herb, tell him the story about that." Then I'd disengage and come back when he was ready. I brought him out of his shell by playing up his skill as a storyteller. My relationship with him was a key factor in becoming his pick to take over.

When we take time to get to know our people, we realize they don't leave jobs just because of the money.

Employees stay because, as leaders, we care about them. It's about showing empathy and kindness and assisting them with figuring out how they can improve their life professionally and personally. I'm a mentor. My door's open all the time. I always have former students and employees come by to check in. It's about building lasting relationships. That's why as leaders we must look to our culture before we randomly blame money as the reason for the resignations.

It's worth your time to sit in the office with every single one of your employees individually, as well as in groups. These meetings have changed since COVID-19. Now we add questions like "Do you want to work from home?" and "Can we have a hybrid model?"

But behind all these questions is one idea: We value you. When's the last time you told your employees that?

Showing your employees you value them is the easiest thing to do. A handwritten note to an employee, a staff barbecue, team events, and recognizing people for good work. It doesn't have to be money all the time. Get creative with it. We got Herby, a rescue dog, because our staff asked, "Why can't we have a dog?" Herby was a great staff morale booster, and a huge member of our team. He is now happily enjoying his retirement, as he should be!

And if the bottom line is something you worry about when doing all this valuing, don't. I told my partners Matt and Kyle (our Corporate Controller) not to worry about the bottom line. To which they all responded, "What are you talking about? That's our success." But I insisted if we looked after our people the bottom line would take care of itself. That opinion has not let me down in my sixteen years at Lexus of Edmonton.

When putting your employees first, the advice is simple: Start with empathy and kindness. If you start with empathy and kindness and show your employees you truly value them, without any lip service, but truly value them, you'll have a lot less people resigning.

THE PURSUIT OF EXCELLENCE

With great people come great rewards—including a ton of industry awards.

Being excellent is easy to do it for a day. It's easy to do it for a week, maybe even a month, but consistently to do it month after month after month—that's a great company. That only happens if your people are trained and believe in your goals. With that, the excellence comes naturally. We empower all our staff here to follow our values, especially at the service desk. Everyone in the Lexus of Edmonton family needs to know and live our DNA.

We also empower them to make their own decisions. I don't want staff running up here with an issue for a hundred dollars. They can make that decision. And if something goes wrong, if a guest is not happy, we empower them to ask what we did wrong. Don't be afraid to ask the guest. Mike, say one of my employees says to you that it's part of our philosophy to make things right and asks, "Mr. Mack, will you please give me the opportunity to make it right?" What are you going to say? Of course, you'll want to give us the chance to make you happy!

The awards are nice, but our reputation is our true success and marker of excellence. The awards only reflect what's already there. It's important for us to judge our success, in order of importance, by answering these questions:

- How happy is our staff?
- What is our reputation with our guests?
- What is our reputation in the community?
- Do we have good staff growth and retention?
- How successful we are in all areas? (And yes, that means profit.)

If we are doing well in all those things, we don't need an award to tell us we're excellent.

NOT A CAR GUY

Matt Miller had been with us for a long time. When he came in to drop off his resume, I was still walking down and accepting each resume personally. Typically, I'd say, "I can't interview today, but I will get back to you." Whether yes or no, I'd get back to them.

I flipped through his resume and noticed he'd gone to university. He played hockey and was captain of his team. He had worked at Earls. He went traveling, which I thought was interesting. I went down to my sales manager, Bob Pinder, who's a car guy (my only car guy) and said, "Matt, I'm going to interview you." I said, "It's a very tough business. If we interview you, you should be ready to explain how you're going to drive your business. That's the toughest part."

Bob goes, "Oh, another non-car guy, right Bruce?"

I go, "Yeah, Bob, another non-car guy."

We interviewed Matt. Near the end of the interview, I said, "You know, Matt, how are you going to drive your own business?" That kid had a one-page business plan. Bob had never seen that. He's kicking me under the table now, saying with his footwear, "This is unbelievable. Unbelievable!" I set it up all perfect.

When the interview was over, Matt wasn't even out the door

before Bob goes, "Don't you think we should hire him, Bruce? I've never seen a kid that knew how to drive his business."

"But Bob, but he's not a car guy." Bob just looked at me with a big smile. I hired Matt.

SPOTTING SUPERSTARS

Matt started as a normal salesman on the floor but right away he did one thing that I'll never forget that showed he was a leader out of the gate. We had a big event called the Sizzling 20 under 30. It was jammed. There were six hundred people in the dealership. When the event was over and everyone had left, the store was still a mess, full of tables and promotional materials and food waste. My detailer and I didn't leave until 1:30 the next morning because we were cleaning up. I was *not* impressed. I wasn't happy with the team, and though I didn't say much to them they could all tell something was wrong.

Later that day I got an email from Matt saying, "I'm sorry, I didn't stay last night. I realized that you do lots to drive our business. It will never happen again; I should have stayed and helped."

I thought, "Wow." And it never did happen again.

I continued to watch Matt grow as I mentored him. Then I decided to promote him to lease manager. Since Matt always wanted to grow and improve, I gave him a monthly book to read to help him on his journey. I remember the time he came into my office when he was the sales manager and asked where his book was. I had forgotten to give it to him that month!

When you're the CEO of your business, you watch people even when they don't think you're watching. And sometimes you watch to discover leaders without a title.

WHEN YOU GOT A GOOD THING, EVERYONE WANTS IT

When you got a good thing, everyone wants it. Over my years in the business, I saw many dealers get their general managers poached from our companies. I'm more of a boutique dealer so I'm very protective of my people and spend numerous hours mentoring them. Not too long after Matt became General Manager, he had Go Auto calling him trying to lure him away. I'm proud that many of my poached staff are general managers at other dealerships, or leaders outside of the automotive industry. It shows me must be doing something right by our employees.

I had a conversation with Matt and told him I'm only one store, so I have limited leadership chairs available. But I also told him if he was patient, we'd get him there. He chose to be patient and loyal and now he has shares in the company. I call him my business partner. The thing is I knew a good thing when I saw it and because I was a small dealership, I had to make sure I protected my people more than the dealerships that had multiple general managers. When it comes to protecting my people, I'm fierce!

COMMUNITY SUPPORT MATTERS

As I learned in my early years, community matters too. Communities are made up of all the people the support your business, so caring for them is key to your success.

In the spring of 2016, a wildfire swept through the northern community of Fort McMurray in northeast Alberta, Canada. Almost 90,000 people were forced from their homes. Sweeping through Fort McMurray, the wildfire destroyed approximately 2,400 homes and buildings.

Fort McMurray is a long way from Edmonton. It takes four and a half hours driving northeast to get there. Right away, I knew we had to do something. I called my management team in and said, "The first thing we need to do today is pull all our Fort McMurray guest names."

We started making calls. How were they doing? What did they need? Can we help? Nothing about their car.

We came up with the idea. We told every guest, "If you need to get out of Fort McMurray right now, and want to come down to Edmonton, we'll arrange for you to stay at a hotel and get a hot meal. And we'll service your car. A gift from Lexus of Edmonton."

On a Friday, we had a barbeque at the store for all the people in Fort McMurray that were in the hotels. I truly believe if there's a disaster, even if it's not part of your business, there's a great opportunity to help your guests, to give, and, as a bonus, expand your reputation. I would hope the idea would come naturally to people, but for many it doesn't. So, this is my time to suggest you get out there and make a difference in people's lives. What opportunity do you have right now in your business to be of value to your clients and community in a way only your business can provide?

The reputation boost is nice, but that wasn't our intention. We didn't offer this help with any hidden agenda. Don't have a hidden agenda when you give, just give. We are extremely involved in the Edmonton community in many areas, and are very proud of that. We are also heavily involved with many charities and events within the city, but we do it for the relationships and because we believe in giving back to our community, not for the recognition. The thing is, when you do good, it comes back to you.

HISTORICAL MENTORS

If I could talk to two people from history, they'd be Steve Jobs and Walt Disney.

I'm amazed at Job's vision of how he built Apple. Also, I'd love to sit down with Walt Disney because I'm such a Disney guy. Disney was absolutely a visionary entrepreneur who struggled to make his dream come true. Even when Disney went bankrupt several times and nobody supported him—even his family thought he was an outcast—he kept going. When you look back at his legacy, created because he never gave up, you can't help but be inspired.

ADVICE FOR YOUNG LEADERS AND ENTREPRENEURS

You'll have heard some of these pieces of advice before, but they're worth repeating.

Make sure you do lots of research and get a mentor. Know, you'll have different mentors along the way at different points in your life.

Have a willingness to learn, and a willingness to fail.

Be decisiveness and passionate.

Foster a strong work ethic.

Make sure you have a good accountant you trust.

Have good relationships at your banks.

Start relationships as early as possible.

Get a good lawyer.

Have a will.

Read, read, read.

Network.

A FINAL WORD ON MENTORS

Entrepreneurs often ask, why would they need a business coach? The short answer is they can make your life better personally and professionally and help you grow. They will push you, support you, challenge you, and provide you with advice.

Never be afraid to ask for help. Find a mentor. Be a lifelong learner.

When I mentor people, at our first meeting I give them three books that they have to read in the next ninety days. Then every year I give them a list of my top ten books. Those aren't just business books. You got to read outside business as well. You need to expand your mind. Get those different pairs of eyes. You could read *Tuesdays with Morrie* and get great insights.

One of the books on my list is *Ego is the Enemy*. I had to give it to one of my people that I was mentoring, to see if he would get the message without me telling him.

We can get blinders on as entrepreneurs and only think about growing ourselves. Grow, sure, but remember you don't run your business alone. If there's one message I want to get across to entrepreneurs, out of everything I've said, it's this: please, please, please invest in your people. They're the best asset you have. Not your building. Not your product. Your people.

Life is all about relationships, Mike. The reason we're both successful is because we're friends and stay connected with each other and so many other people. People need to get out more and connect with others. I'm blessed to have you. I mean, everybody in this town talks so highly of you, Mike. You and your company have an amazing reputation that you should be proud of. I wouldn't hesitate to make an introduction for you to support a business with the coaching services you provide at X5 Management.

As leaders, we need to focus on the little things in our business as we do the big things right. As entrepreneurs and leaders, we focus too much time and energy on the big things. We here at Lexus of Edmonton focus more on the little things—every touch point is an opportunity.

Everything counts, but the little things can have an outsized impact on success, both in business and in life.

A DEDICATION AND MESSAGE FROM MIKE

Below, you'll see a very special photo for Bruce, for many reasons. He fondly has it placed in his office.

These great men were a huge part of Bruce's life, both personally and professionally.

In 2021, Herb Anton, Founder of Lexus of Edmonton, passed away at the age of 91. Only a year later, in the summer of 2022, Matt Miller, Dealer Principal, tragically lost his life in an accident. Matt was 42 years old.

This chapter is dedicated to the memories of both fine men who had a tremendous impact on Bruce, the entire Lexus of Edmonton team, and their community. They made a difference and always put People First.

L-R: Bruce Kirkland, Herb Anton, and Matt Miller

Bruce Kirkland is President and CEO of Lexus of Edmonton. He was born in McLennan, Alberta, and started day one at Lexus of Edmonton in 2004. Bruce loves to travel and comes from a family of 11; he is lucky number 7. Bruce believes in being a life-long learner.

5

Big Business is No Small Potatoes

Angela Santiago and The Little Potato Company

THE LITTLE POTATO COMPANY IS A LOCAL BUSIness success story. Over the past 11 years I have driven by The Little Potato company on my way to work with a valued client every week. Years back, my curiosity got the best of me, and I had to try their product in a local grocery store; I'm a fan of supporting local where possible.

As a member of the business community, I came across two opportunities to hear their CEO, Angela Santiago, present. I was so impressed with her business savvy and the calm confidence in the words that she shared. She's an impressive entrepreneur and a most astute and compassionate businesswoman.

When I was planning the concept of *Lunch with Leaders*, I knew that Angela had to be part of the book. The catch: I didn't know Angela—but fortunately, my professional network is strong. I reached out to a friend and fellow member of Synergy Network, Dan Duckering, and Dan was quick to offer an introduction. Before I knew it, Angela had agreed to a virtual call with me. I am delighted to have her contribution as part of the book.

What I found unique about Angela during our interview process is that her words literally fell onto the page with very little editing or clarification needed. She is a well-spoken and incredibly articulate business leader.

Angela is well known by the business community as an authentic and genuine leader.

Enjoy Angela's incredible entrepreneurial journey.

EARLY AMBITIONS

Funny story: I dreamt of being a jockey, because I loved horses. However, I grew to be 5'10", so that was completely out of the cards for me. Interestingly, I was the student council president in my senior year. As part of the election process, they conducted a bio interview. I came across it many years later and remembered saying, "Oh, I'd love to own my own business," when I was 18. Of course, I went on to university and completely forgot what I said at 18. It was an interesting note for me to realize that even at that age, I had the idea of running my own business. That discovery gave me pause for reflection.

When I reflect on the stories that run through our family, involving my parents, my brothers, myself, and my four children, the entrepreneurial spirit of my parents had a profound effect on us. I grew up in a business atmosphere, which I thought was totally normal. Looking back, my aspirations at 18 stemmed from what I believed was possible. I consider it a privilege to have had parents who were entrepreneurial and eager to explore life and figure things out.

A POTATO DREAM IS BORN

Witnessing a very entrepreneurial spirit in both my parents, I was encouraged to attend post-secondary school in Edmonton, where I earned my business diploma as well as a political science degree with a minor in history. When I was graduating from the University of Alberta, my dad introduced another business idea about small potatoes. It's heartwarming because this idea stemmed from his childhood memories of growing up in the Netherlands and picking the little potatoes off the field.

The funny thing is, these little potatoes were the delicious ones. However, they were usually left behind in the field by harvesters and were often just plowed over afterward. Yet these were the ones locals would pick up and cook at home. My father cherished the memories of picking them and how tasty they were.

The magic moment occurred when he recalled this memory while sitting in a small truck stop cafe outside of Edmonton. At that time, he overheard some Dutch potato farmers conversing. My dad and I were doing taping and drywall together to support my education.

What was magical was that these Dutch farmers were speaking Frisian—a language from the northern part of the Netherlands spoken by maybe only a few million people worldwide. It felt like the stars were aligning.

Hearing these gentlemen talk about small potatoes, my dad exclaimed, "What?" That conversation sparked the big idea for small potatoes. Bursting with excitement, he approached me at our job site and shared, "I overheard these guys talking about small potatoes. I remember them from my youth. I wonder if there's a business idea here?" As a typical 20-year-old, I was skeptical. He suggested, "Why don't you help me start this?" Though I hesitated, I eventually agreed. At the time, I couldn't envision a future in agriculture, especially not in potatoes. After all, who pursues that as a career?

WASHING POTATOES AT THE CAR WASH

It's so surreal to discuss this, but here we are, 27 years later, and I'm sitting in front of you, Mike, talking about The Little Potato Company. Clearly, I never pursued anything else!

I'm so grateful I didn't. In the early years, we planted the potatoes by hand, on our hands and knees, on some borrowed land outside of Edmonton. The first harvest was also done manually, using buckets and makeshift harnesses we strapped to our bodies. Our goal was to improve our methods, so we wouldn't have to keep selling at the local farmer's market after washing the potatoes in a bathtub! Although rudimentary, these initial steps provided a valuable learning experience, and the feedback we received propelled us to invest in old, worn-out equipment. Our aim was to devise better washing methods than the bathtub. First, we tried a car wash, then moved on to an old, rusty barrel washer. I can attest to the fact that we were deeply involved in every aspect, from planting to nurturing our venture, both literally and figuratively, from the ground up.

Fast forward to today: it's been twenty-seven years. While I might have entered this business somewhat reluctantly and unintentionally, I choose to remain here with purpose and intent. I adore the food industry, and I cherish the humility that comes from producing and providing food for others. Working with something as basic as a potato—which isn't a novel concept, considering its age-old presence—is intriguing. Taking such a traditional item and innovating around it, while still feeding people, offers a profound sense of fulfillment.

Our company's mission is to "feed the world better." This purpose is precisely why I remain so committed and passionate about the company and why I have cherished leading it for the past 27 years.

BECOMING A LEADER

Going back to my roots as a young 20-something, there's a part of you at that age that wants to conquer the world. However, there's also a part of you that has no idea how you're going to achieve that or how you'll contribute to the world.

Making significant decisions at such an age is intriguing. I've learned, even when advising my kids, that everything is fluid. The choices you make now might not reflect what you'll be doing 15 or 20 years later. They're important decisions, but they aren't definitive.

My journey into leadership stemmed from the fact that, at that age, I didn't recognize all that I was or could become.

The wonderful part is that, all along the way, many key individuals, including my parents and especially my dad, recognized my leadership potential. They saw my capability to steer a company successfully. I believe my leadership emerged organically, fuelled by people who saw potential in me that I perhaps didn't recognize in myself.

I pass this important lesson onto my children. I observe qualities in them that they might not yet recognize. However, my leadership journey wasn't instantaneous; I didn't simply wake up one day seeing myself as the CEO. Anyone who has started a company from scratch understands that in the throes of building, you often don't perceive yourself as a leader. My leadership evolved gradually, bolstered by abundant encouragement and support.

SCALING OPPORTUNITIES

I have a few stories related to scaling up. In the very beginning, we focused on food service, but I'll say that it quickly changed direction. We were selling only at the farmer's market at that time. Why was that important? A chef recognized that these potatoes were special. It was a feather in our cap to offer them, suggesting that we were onto something. What followed soon after was a listing with the IGA stores in Alberta.

The IGA story is quite unique. It began with me cold calling a buyer. After several attempts, I secured an appointment. We met the gentleman in the stairway before the reception. There, in that stairway, we presented our product to him. We mentioned, "We have about 30,000 pounds of this. It's not much." To which he replied, "I'll take it all." Just like that, our entire crop was sold in that rather understated meeting.

After that encounter, we realized, "Holy crap, we are onto something." Next, we worked with Safeway, secured the Loblaw private label, and partnered with Costco. All the major retailers in Canada showed support, acknowledging, "Yes, this is a great product." These milestones truly resonate with me from a business standpoint. However, numerous behind-the-scenes events and lessons, especially those about finding trustworthy individuals, were crucial for me. Over 27 years, a select group of people have significantly impacted the company. After acquiring our first US customer, securing Walmart as a partner was a significant milestone for us in the US, leading to the construction of our facility there.

HOW TO KNOCK ON DOORS—AND GET IN

Here's a charming story. We were at a trade show in the US when a representative from Walmart visited our booth. They noticed our product and mentioned having seen it in markets. At that time, we had made a strong entrance into the Northeast, particularly the Boston-New York area. The Walmart buyer asked, "Why haven't you approached us?" I responded, "Well, because we're intimidated by you." He laughed and inquired, "Why would you be intimidated?" I explained, "Given your company's size and influence." He reassured me, saying, "Don't worry about it. We'll guide you through the process." And that's exactly what they did. Walmart, despite its colossal stature, gently introduced us to their system. Over time, we expanded to supply all their stores, but we approached the distribution growth cautiously.

We never arrogantly declared, "We can handle your demand without a hitch."

It was quite the opposite. We acknowledged, "We understand the scale of your operations, and here's our limited capacity. We have a fantastic product but are uncertain about distributing it at your volume."

I cherish this anecdote because it emphasizes two principles: first, to avoid making presumptions and second, the value of candor. When you adhere to these principles, it's astounding what opportunities can present themselves, even with giants like Walmart.

HOW TO DEAL WITH HUMANS

Always be authentic and honest about your company's capabilities with retailers; you'd be surprised at how well they relate to it.

Similarly, when we started Loblaw's private label, it took off much faster than either party had anticipated. We had forecasted for six months but reached that volume in just six weeks. As you can imagine, it was chaotic behind the scenes. I vividly recall an early morning call with the buyer in Toronto due to the time difference. I was in the stairway of my house, so nervous about this conversation. I thought, "Well, it is what it is." The crux of our conversation was that we couldn't manage the volume we were experiencing. This volume was anticipated over six months, yet it happened in six weeks.

I share this with you because the same approach worked on both sides of the border.

We're humans on both sides. Honesty and authenticity aren't determined by country but by our shared humanity. I cherish this story as it was a profound learning experience.

WHAT TO DO WHEN YOU HEAR "NO"

When we first entered the U.S., we had a meeting with a couple of retailers on the Pacific Northwest side. They immediately said, "No thank you."

We said, "Well, okay," and we went back to Canada. One piece of feedback I received early on, and I'm glad I received it early, was, "You Canadians just take no for an answer. You should keep coming back and asking again." That advice was invaluable for a Canadian company entering the U.S. That's how we acquired many of our customers afterward; we didn't take "no" for an answer. We tried again and again until we secured their business.

THE AMERICAN MARKET

That was also the strategy we used to get Costco USA as a customer. We just went back and continued to knock, knock, knock. We'd say, "I know you said 'not yet.'" And this is a significant difference. Americans do expect you to be a little more aggressive and not take "no" for an answer.

The thing is, we're so different in Canada that we very quickly hired American salespeople because of the language and shared history they have. The connections and history come from all directions, whether they're related to sports, where they grew up, or where they went to school. And that kind of history cannot be replicated by someone who hasn't experienced it.

That was another valuable lesson: although there are aspects that are very similar, there are differences, and you must recognize them. So, we quickly hired people who were born and raised in the US to handle sales.

EXPANDING IN THE USA

You must understand your target market. That was really a key part of our success in the US. I had a very capable VP of Sales who understood this very well. In Canada, what's considered regional here is seen as national. It's crucial to grasp this concept. For instance, the volume a Texan retailer might handle could be comparable to that of a national retailer in Canada. If you don't understand that, you're in for a surprise.

That's why we divided our approach and began in two regions.

One was the Northeast, encompassing areas like New York and Boston, supplied by our PEI growing region and PEI plant. Then there was the Pacific Northwest and California, served by our Edmonton plant. Even though it's all one country, you segment it by region, as if each region is its own country. This strategy was beneficial, but as many of these retailers expanded, our freight lanes became increasingly extensive.

FARMERS AS PARTNERS

Currently, we cultivate around 14,000 acres. The majority are in three regions. First, there's Alberta and Saskatchewan. We have some areas around Edmonton and in Southern Alberta and Saskatchewan, and these growing regions supply the Edmonton plant. Our second major growing region is in Prince Edward Island, with a bit in Nova Scotia. The third primary growing area is in Wisconsin. Additionally, we have a growing region in Washington that aids with 12 months of supply. As we expanded, our focus was on pinpointing the best regions for potato cultivation since potatoes are selective about their growing conditions. They prefer long, warm days and cool nights and are not fans of intense heat. This rules out many areas.

This aligns with the importance of starting small. We began with 50 acres, allowing the grower to become accustomed to the process. One shouldn't initiate with 300 acres and anticipate everything to run smoothly.

All our growers operate family farms. Interestingly, not all of them began as small potato farmers. Some hadn't even cultivated potatoes before partnering with us. I cherish the collaboration with family farms. They are genuinely passionate about feeding other families, which aligns perfectly with our company values and our mission to serve the world and consumers.

BUILDING UNDER THE RADAR

I went from being an outsider to a leader. That transition was a significant challenge and journey. I was perceived as an outsider because I didn't have a background in potatoes, wasn't part of the industry, had no agricultural experience, and was entering a realm set in its traditional ways. However, being an outsider also presented certain advantages.

For years, I was overlooked. As frustrating as that was, the silver lining was that people didn't keep tabs on me. This allowed me to quietly and diligently build a company under the radar.

Like every entrepreneur, securing financing for a start-up presented challenges, with banks often expressing skepticism. Additionally, being a female in a predominantly male, traditional industry added another layer of complexity. The landscape is shifting now, but 26 years ago, I frequently found myself as the only woman in the room.

BALANCE OVER A LIFETIME

You don't, and I didn't either. I have an amazing partner, Frank, who has been my biggest cheerleader and support to help balance the family. It's a team effort. I think another significant challenge was juggling the personal side, becoming a new wife, having four kids, and trying to grow a business. Those were some of the most difficult years of my life. Often, I'd end the day feeling that I hadn't done anything well: not being an attentive and present mom, the business not being completely in order, and not feeling like an attentive wife.

Those, for me at the beginning, were very real challenges of growing a business and being an entrepreneur. We all know when you run your own business, it doesn't turn off. You don't get to just lock it up at the end of the day; you take it all home.

I think another challenge in the business part was that we were trying to establish a new category within a very traditional one. Some retailers easily understood it. They got it right away. For others, it was a significant shift. It took a long time to get some retailers on board, but that's also the exciting part of innovation: doing that work and getting people to change their perspective. So, while it might not seem like a lengthy list of challenges, they were very significant and very real for me.

Maria Schriver once shared words in an interview with Oprah that truly resonated with me. I won't quote her verbatim, but she essentially said, "Balance will come over time and over a lifetime. It won't come in a day or a week or even a year; sometimes, you just won't have balance."

I've definitely experienced that. When all my kids were young and I was trying to build a business, I felt completely off-balance. There was a period when the business completely dominated my life. Now, the pendulum has swung back. I feel much more balanced and spend more intentional time with my family, husband, and kids. I've truly lived her words.

It's crucial to see life as a balancing act because if you don't, you'll be very hard on yourself. Balance often doesn't come naturally, especially for entrepreneurs. By default, our autopilot mode is work. We love it and derive immense value from it. The second lesson I've learned is the importance of being intentional and planning meticulously. From budgeting and strategizing in business to ensuring quality family time, all require careful thought and execution.

BALANCE YOUR BUCKETS

I couldn't do it by myself. One of the analogies I've shared with many entrepreneurs is "buckets." I put this on a big board that I see every day when I walk out of my room. The categories are family, work, business, and life. It serves as a momentary pause for me to assess: where am I running on empty among these buckets?

Often, one would be completely overflowing. Then I'd look at the other buckets and realize I haven't taken care of myself, or I haven't taken care of my family or my marriage. It's just a pause to consider which bucket is depleting. Over the years, I've learned that when a bucket is on "E", it typically spells disaster.

A WILLINGNESS TO LEARN

For me, the greatest achievement wouldn't make the front-page news. It's building strong, trusted, loyal relationships both internally and externally. Also, within the industry, we've had growers with us almost from the very beginning. I've had retailers with us from almost the start, and some of the same buyers are still with us. These are the types of "behind the scenes" accomplishments that don't make the front-page news. In terms of the significant rewards of growing a business, I'd point to all the incredible learnings I've had—much of which you can't find in a textbook or obtain from a degree. The willingness to learn is so powerful.

STAYING MOTIVATED WHEN IT GETS TOUGH

One of the things I'm most proud of is the creation of a category that never existed before us. I'll share a story about my brother, which he probably doesn't recall. It happened on a day when I was facing challenges with one of our breeding partners in Europe. It was a discouraging day, one of those moments where I questioned my choices. My brother remarked, "Angela, no matter what happens, nobody can undo or take away what you and dad have accomplished." He was spot on. We pioneered a category, and once that bell was rung, it couldn't be un-rung. Even if we chose to close our doors, the category of little potatoes would remain in the market. That realization is truly phenomenal.

Another unseen reward comes from the letters, emails, and comments I receive from consumers across Canada and the US. They often share sentiments like, "We love your potatoes. Here's what I did with them." These messages resonate deeply with me and are one of the primary reasons I'm driven to continue. I like to envision our produce ending up on someone's plate, nourishing their family. The very act of someone purchasing our product in a store, whether in New York or Florida, and taking the time to write a letter of appreciation is deeply gratifying. These rewards have nothing to do with a Profit and Loss statement or store shelf space. It's all about the intrinsic satisfaction of serving people.

ALL ABOUT BRANDING

When it comes to branding the business, there's a funny story that many people aren't aware of. Our company's first incorporated name was "Gourmet Produce." At the time, we thought it was a fantastic name. So, we proceeded, created bags, and started selling. Later on, we received a letter from a lawyer stating that "Gourmet Produce" had been trademarked in relation to vegetables. We were instructed to cease and desist from using that name. Naturally, we felt as though it was the end of the world.

However, I often believe that such "end of the world" challenges can spark new beginnings!

We began brainstorming, involving the shareholders and all of our significant others. "The Little Potato Company" emerged as the chosen name. This experience taught us that adversity can sometimes lead to better outcomes, and from then on, we never looked back.

That's not to say our brand hasn't evolved over the years. Our target market has shifted, but "The Little Potato Company" has consistently remained our name. Over time, our approach to marketing has become much more sophisticated. There's a common misconception that marketing is merely about appealing packaging, catchy phrases, and advertisements. In reality, effective marketing involves measurable metrics and intentional processes supported by thorough research. Our journey to understanding and applying these principles has been incredibly rewarding. Currently, we are in the process of undergoing another rebrand.

FINDING INSPIRATION

I know many people draw inspiration from historical figures, but I find mine in everyday people who face hardships and figure out how to overcome them. The individuals who show up consistently, without any special pedigree or acclaim, inspire me. They haven't written a book or made a historical impact. It's simply their dedication to showing up and doing their work that I find inspiring. Mike, I love sitting down with such people. I enjoy conversations with workers at our plant, other entrepreneurs, and our staff.

ENTREPRENEURIAL WEAKNESSES

Two weaknesses come to mind right away. Even this far into my career, with twenty-seven years of growing a business, I doubt myself and my capabilities. I don't often take the time to tell myself, "You did pretty good here, Angela."

The second weakness is that I'm too nice and patient, which often results in delays. Although I'm getting much better at it, I have sometimes postponed necessary, courageous conversations with people about performance or about what I need from them. I tend to give people second and third chances. This approach has often worked in my favour, but not always. When it hasn't, there have been significant consequences.

ENTREPRENEURIAL SUPERPOWER

My superpower is my heart and that I love and care for people. And I think the other piece is my resilience. I somehow always figure it out. Might have not been Plan A, might be Plan B or C, but I certainly don't give up I always find a way to do it. Also, I love looking long-term, thinking 10 years out. I get a lot of excitement from that.

INCESSANT CURIOSITY

I believe there are certain characteristics people are born with that make them more inclined to become entrepreneurs. This doesn't necessarily guarantee that they will become entrepreneurs, but there are definite traits.

Incessant curiosity is one such trait, along with resilience, drive, and self-motivation.

When I look at myself and my two brothers, we are very different, yet we are all entrepreneurial. I attribute this to our upbringing and how we were encouraged and supported. You might be born with a few of these traits, but you don't need to inherit them to become an entrepreneur. Watching my parents take risks rather than always playing it safe gave us the permission to make our own mistakes and learn from them.

If you have a support system that allows you to take such risks and learn, then I believe anyone can be entrepreneurial.

EMBRACE VULNERABILITY TO SHINE

I truly love people, their growth, and their personal journey. These journeys don't necessarily begin and end with our company. Perhaps they intersect with us for a brief period, but we genuinely root for their success, with no strings attached. I believe that's what defines a great leader and a great entrepreneur.

We are all human, shaped by our past experiences. The distinction between a good leader and a great one lies in their willingness to confront and address their personal challenges. By this, I mean that we should lead holistically. Our personal challenges, traumas, and unresolved issues from the past will inevitably surface, especially in leadership roles.

Leaders who are prepared to confront these issues, who embrace vulnerability and self-love, truly shine. When they acknowledge their limitations, they create space for others to contribute and fill in the gaps. Conversely, if you present yourself as infallible, you leave no room for others to support or add value to your efforts. This mindset, I believe, is crucial.

The constant desire to learn and maintain curiosity leaves little room for ego. When you're always in the mindset of "I don't know, but I'd like to" or "I don't know, let's find out," you're emphasizing the importance of growth and knowledge. Being perpetually curious, whether about personal growth or general knowledge, minimizes judgment and keeps the ego in check.

SUCCESSION PLANNING

There are two flows of work here, and this topic is very near and dear to my heart. I'll delve into some details about what I did in response. Being the majority owner of the company and its only CEO, many associate me closely with Angela and The Little Potato Company. When I consider the company's longevity and its dedicated employees who depend on it for their income, I feel a deep sense of responsibility and moral obligation to ensure there's a contingency plan should something happen to me.

I collaborated with one of my advisory board members on this endeavor, and I'm grateful for her assistance. Initially, I assumed the process would be straightforward and that there might be a pre-existing template for such a plan. However, after an extensive search yielded no results, we created one. This plan begins with an immediate 90-day strategy.

The initial actions, to be taken within the first 24-72 hours, are laid out clearly, detailing how we'd commence the search for my successor. The plan is comprehensive and highly effective. Running parallel to this is the acknowledgment that the company hasn't just lost a family member, but also a leader. The plan outlines the subsequent steps to be taken.

PARALLEL PLANNING

There is a parallel 60-day plan for the family, outlining what needs to be done during a crisis. Everyone will be alright, and the company will persevere. It was crucial for me to document and outline this, as I feel a sense of duty towards those who dedicate themselves to both me and the company daily. The plan ensures continuity and stability, preventing any abrupt dissolution or disruption. Additionally, I'm currently engaged in developing a family succession governance plan alongside my brothers, which I find immensely enjoyable. We've partnered with an exceptional facilitator from Vancouver Island who is highly experienced in this domain.

This aspect of planning addresses the inevitable aging process, and the challenges and considerations that come with it. Given that all of us have children, we discuss how to navigate situations where family members wish to retain ownership without taking on managerial roles. We're also exploring how best to transition ownership and responsibility to our children.

Being naturally inclined towards organization and planning, I felt a deep-seated responsibility not only to my corporate family at Little Potato Company but also to my immediate family. My objective was to provide clarity for both.

I urge fellow business owners to prioritize such planning. Through my collaboration with experts in this field, I've become aware of instances where the absence of a succession plan led to severe family rifts. Our guiding principle has always been that family relationships are paramount, even more so than the business. Engaging in these discussions while all stakeholders are present and actively participating is, in my opinion, the best approach to safeguard our familial bonds, ensuring they remain intact and unaffected.

MISSED OPPORTUNITIES

I believe there were times I moved too quickly to notice them! My missed opportunity, I'd say, was not recognizing those warning signs earlier in life. I found myself in a health crisis, and had I taken better care of myself, I might not have overlooked the signs that presented themselves along the way. Trust me, those signs do appear. There were definite missed opportunities in terms of self-care for me. By always being on the go, there were actions I could have taken more deliberately, which might have led to different business decisions.

BUCKET LIST ITEMS

Some items on my bucket list align with our purpose, which is "feed the world better."

I've always felt a deep urge to provide better food for people. You can discuss this with my dad, as well as my brothers who are now involved in the business. Moreover, a significant number of our company's employees genuinely embrace this belief, as it's the foundational principle of our company.

Everyone requires food and water, but we believe that all individuals, regardless of their location, should have access to healthy, quality food. Our core philosophy is that no one should go without food. One of my aspirations is to collaborate with the UN on food security, ensuring that I can further the mission of The Little Potato Company on a larger scale.

The concept of leading from a distance appeals to me.

Being detached from minute details grants me the freedom to apply what I've learned over the past twenty-seven years. I adore the idea of traveling more with my husband and children. I love road trips. I love Europe.

TRAVEL WISHLIST

I'd love to travel by caravan throughout Europe. My husband and I enjoy experiencing a country by driving through it. This would undoubtedly be one of the activities I'd cherish doing with my family. We always have a great time when we rent a house in a warm location, with just us and a pool. We don't make many plans, and I appreciate that simplicity.

Mike, I also want to express my gratitude for giving me the opportunity to reflect on my journey. I understand it's for your book, but for an entrepreneur, or anyone with a busy schedule, taking a moment to contemplate topics like this is immensely impactful.

I'm eager to hear the stories of others. There's immense value in learning how individuals surmount their challenges and the life lessons they derive from those experiences.

Angela Santiago co-founded The Little Potato Company Ltd. with her father, Jacob Vander Schaaf, a Dutch immigrant who longed for the tasty 'little potatoes' of his youth.

After graduating from the University of Alberta with a Political Science Degree and eyes on a political career, Angela was intrigued when her entrepreneurial father asked her to help bring his idea of little potatoes to fruition. In 1996, the two began with a one-acre plot of little potatoes—grown and washed by hand to sell at local farmers' markets. Local chefs, consumers, and retailers loved the potatoes so much that the little company soon grew. Today, partnered with family farms across North America, The Little Potato Company potatoes are sold in more than 20,000 stores across Canada and the USA.

Angela has earned honors from a number of organizations, including: Top Produce Person of the Year (Ontario Provincial Marketing Association); Top Forty Under Forty in Canada (2011); Entrepreneur of the Year Award

(Ernst & Young, 2012); Business in Edmonton Leader (2015); Alberta's Woman Entrepreneur of the Year (2016); Top 10 Produce Women in Canada (2021); Top Women in Grocery Award (Progressive Grocer, 2021); and King's University Distinguished Alumni Award (2021).

6

Let Go to Grow

Shannon Waller and Strategic Coach®

HANNON WALLER IS ONE OF THOSE UNIQUE individuals who makes you feel better simply by having a conversation with her. She built her insight into leadership and entrepreneurship over thirty-two years of progressive responsibility at Strategic Coach®, a business coaching organization run by entrepreneurs for entrepreneurs.

Years back, I was a client of Strategic Coach® and gained a tremendous amount of value from the entrepreneurial program. I would go to Vancouver every quarter and spend time with other entrepreneurs. During that time, I learned of Shannon Waller and was blessed to have Shannon support me as a business coach, and I enjoyed many "sounding board calls" with her. I was honored to have Shannon agree to be part of my book.

MY ROLE AT STRATEGIC COACH®

I play several different roles at Strategic Coach®. I'm on the senior leadership team and work very closely with co-founders Dan Sullivan and Babs Smith. Dan is the visionary for the program, and Babs is the visionary for the company. The two top roles I play in the company are Dan's creative collaborator and Babs's strategic partner.

I'm also the creator of the Strategic Coach® Team Programs, or what we call Team+, which has created an additional arm of our business. I'm also a speaker, presenter, coach, and team leader. I coach onsite workshops as well as our 10x Ambition Program™ workshops. Essentially, the thing that suits me most is "front stage," the more the better.

HOW I GOT INVOLVED WITH STRATEGIC COACH®

I started with Strategic Coach® in July of 1991 at the age of twenty-six. I initially met Dan and Babs when I worked for a management consulting company, and I was the administrator of four of the major training programs for General Motors of Canada where Strategic Coach® used to rent seminar room space.

Right away, I noticed Coach clients were quite different from the usual clients we hosted. They were much more open and friendly with one another. Now that I look back, I think this was because they were entrepreneurs rather than the corporate people we typically dealt with.

I went to see Dan give an introductory talk about the program. Long story short, a salesperson called me and said, "What did you think of Dan's talk and the presentation?"

I said, "I loved it. Dan put together things I had known about, but not integrated that way."

Her second question was timeless and beautiful: "Are you happy with what you're doing?"

Out of my mouth popped, "No, I'm bored."

Five weeks later, I was on board with Coach as a salesperson.

HOW I BEGAN COACHING

Eventually, I built my own sales team. After three years, I thought my brain was going to rust, so I went back to school and did a Training and Design Certificate Program from what was then Ryerson University. For one of the course requirements, I came up with the idea for a one-day program for team members of our clients. When I told Babs about it, she said, "Great, let's do it!" I love that my coaching career is essentially the by-product of a school project.

But now, I'd have to take an idea and put it into action. In the beginning, I didn't know how to design a workshop, so Dan designed my first few until I realized I had to do my own design, not his. I went into the workshop room to rehearse before my first workshop. I remember walking up to the front of the room, opening my mouth, and nothing came out. I was like, "Oh, I actually don't know how I'm going to start this!"

I went back, got some things prepared, successfully delivered the workshop, and it took off from there. That evolved into designing and coaching more Strategic Coach® Team Programs for assistants, team members, and team leaders and involving other coaches as well.

WHAT STRATEGIC COACH® DOES FOR ENTREPRENEURS

We help entrepreneurs think about how to run their businesses and lives differently. In other words, we're a mindset company—we help you think about your thinking. I love Dan's way of describing what Coach offers: Unique Concepts—thinking tools; Unique Conversations—with yourself and others; and Unique Community—of like-minded, growth-oriented, talented, ambitious, creative, and collaborative entrepreneurs. This really sums it up, and it happens in workshops, in between sessions on our Connection Calls, and in conversations with our team. It's not just the four quarterly workshops—it's a year-round experience.

Entrepreneurs are not your everyday businesspeople. As Dan likes to say, approximately five percent of the working population are entrepreneurs, and we work with five percent of that five percent. Entrepreneurs are willing to cross what we call the "risk line" from the "time and effort" economy and operate in the "results economy."

Our purpose, our reason for being, is to expand entrepreneurial success, freedom, and happiness.

And we do that really, really well. So, we've got mindsets, we've got programs, we've got community, we've got books, we've got all the things to help entrepreneurs achieve those goals.

THE FOUR FREEDOMS DEFINED

When we talk about expanding freedom, we're very focused on the Four Freedoms of time, money, relationship, and purpose.

Freedom of Time means doing more of what you love to do, less of what you don't, and taking time off to rejuvenate.

Freedom of Money is necessary because freedom costs a lot of money, so you need to be able to pay for it and to have no ceiling on your income.

Freedom of Relationship means working with the people you want to work with, both in terms of your clientele as well as your team—being able to attract and keep great talent.

Freedom of Purpose means you're freed up to have the impact you're passionate about having on the world—making the difference you want to make and living true to yourself.

That's what we help our clients do. Since 1989, we have helped over 20,000 entrepreneurs in sixty different industries around the world achieve faster growth, greater profits, and an exceptional quality of life.

Our reach is ever expanding. In addition to having offices in Toronto, Chicago, and Los Angeles, we have an office in England and work with hundreds of global entrepreneurs there. We've been around for over thirty years, which shows not only our longevity, but how much we enjoy coaching in whatever form it takes. We're excited to see where the whole new virtual world will take the company and our clients.

FINDING SUPERSTARS IN A SKY FULL OF STARS, OR DELEGATION DEATH TRAPS

To be a leader, you must have people to lead.

The number-one challenge for entrepreneurs is getting those people at the beginning and recognizing the superstars. I was recently interviewed for a podcast and asked to describe my very first hire. At the time, I was sharing a part-time person with a colleague, and at first, when I was asked to take over this part-time person by myself, I was terrified. But I made the leap, and after three weeks, I asked how soon she could go full-time, the leverage was so great.

Part of making that first hire was acknowledging that yes, I am a rugged individualist, but no, I can't and shouldn't be doing everything by myself. So, I needed to hire someone so I could get greater leverage and growth for my company. But I needed to hire the right people who were highly skilled in those areas that I'm not.

Most people reading this book are probably already leaders, but they have trouble letting go. I use a racing baton to demonstrate this: like in a relay, you need to have a good handoff to the right person to win the race. The problem is, they've got a very tight grip on certain activities. We call it the *delegation death grip*. They've let it go, supposedly, but really they're still holding on. The other person's trying to pull it, and they're not letting go.

It could come down to a lack of trust, a lack of confidence, or a lack of communication. You've essentially got two people trying to do the job, which is very inefficient and unprofitable. I like to say, "Let go to grow." One of my clients made a personalized racing baton for our team with this inscribed on it and sent me one, which is a fun reminder.

Once a leader decides to let go, it helps the people underneath them grow. This way, you keep strengthening the next layer of leadership and capability in your organization.

On the opposite end is another delegation mishap, the *drive-by delegation*. This happens when you whip an idea at someone's head and run away, not giving them an opportunity to talk it through with you or ask questions. We think we've delegated, but all we've really done is leave someone holding a task or project with no idea what to do. Not good.

THE BIGGEST OBSTACLE IN THE WORKPLACE

I find drama in the workplace to be the biggest distraction of time, money, and emotion and one of the worst leadership situations. This drama is what caused me to write the book *Multiplication by Subtraction: How to Gracefully Let Go of Wrong-Fit Team Members*.

As leaders, we often don't see the problems. The rest of the team might know someone's terrible, toxic, not pulling their weight, or just cares about themselves, but we don't see the signs. We're the last ones to know.

One example was James. He had his "#1 guy" on his team who was supposed to work with me and the rest of his team. And this #1 only paid us lip service and was so inauthentic and fake. I said, "James, that guy's here for his reasons, not yours," but James didn't see it.

Two-and-a-half years later, James says, "You know what? That conversation we had—you were right about him."

I'm like, "I know!" I didn't use the phrase, "I told you so," but I was close enough.

It took James over two years to realize his mistake because the other guy was very smart. By the time he was gone, he had ownership in the company. Essentially, he was kingdom-building—carving out his own little piece of turf. I don't think James wanted to admit it. So, he got suckered by someone who was a strong leader in some ways, but not a leader for the company. #1 was only a leader for himself, which is never good for a company.

James had a blind spot when it came to his #1 guy. The guy was super intelligent, spoke the language, talked the talk, but it was a values issue. He wasn't there for the right reason. His *why* wasn't the same *why* as the owner, and it was a mess. It was costly on a few different fronts. Clients went away. It was sad. The problem with #1 was clear to me because of my filters, but not so obvious to James.

Blind spots are interesting, because...well...you can't see them!

WHAT IS A BLIND SPOT?

A blind spot amounts to assuming the rest of the world operates like you do, and every single one of us does this at some point. What is so obvious and easy for us, we assume is obvious and easy for other people. Not true.

There are many ways blind spots come into the picture:

- We assume the same values.
- We assume the same Kolbe. (Assessment tool used by Strategic Coach®)
- We assume the same strengths.

We think other people are tweaked versions of us. Unless we deeply know someone, which takes a long time, we assume that our filters about them are accurate. And often we are so driven by what we want that we ignore signs to the contrary.

Then there's the fact we've never run into a person like this before. We've never run into that circumstance, and we just don't know. It's not stupidity, but it is ignorance. And our opportunity is to learn from that circumstance, so it doesn't happen again. There may not have been a whole lot we could have done to prevent it; it was just one of the bumps in the road we had to overcome.

THE BEST WAY TO DEAL WITH AN "I TOLD YOU SO"

Like James, we've all been here before. Someone forewarned you about someone or some situation and you failed to heed their advice. Or, in other words, you didn't listen.

The leadership failure with #1, from my standpoint, was not that something happened. It was when it kept happening and James didn't change his approach. It's vital to learn from mistakes the first time.

From an entrepreneurial leadership standpoint, in terms of hiring and team building, you want to look at the three parts of the mind: cognitive (thinking), affective (feeling), and conative (doing). You can ask yourself:

- Does the person have the right intellect?
- Does the person have the right striving instincts for the role? (This is what the Kolbe A™ profile measures)
- Does the person have the right values?

The type of situation that happened to James frankly ticks me off. The third time it happened, I was like, "Seriously? Come on." I was annoyed enough to write *Multiplication by Subtraction*. I tend to write books when I'm mad. It's a good impetus for me. I see something out there and it's like, "Oh, I don't want this to happen to anybody else." I want people to go from fake to fabulous.

INVEST IN FABULOUS

When you get someone who is fabulous, invest in them like crazy. You've got someone who—if they're smart; if they're applying their knowledge; if they're there for the company's reasons, not just their own; and if they've got the right instincts for the role— is going to be a spectacular contributor to your company. And maybe they'll get to a certain level of success and go no further, but at least you'll have a winner.

I make a distinction between entrepreneurial and bureaucratic. Bureaucracies encourage and attract people who are status oriented. Entrepreneurial organizations focus on something different. I prefer the motto, "Always make your contribution greater than your status." As far as I'm concerned, status is a by-product of contribution. My status at Coach is strictly a result of my contribution, and the day that that changes, I should get the heck out of there.

NO ONE CAN READ YOUR MIND,
SO COMMUNICATE RESULTS CLEARLY

All humans want you to read their minds, but especially entrepreneurs because they move so darned fast. I used to jokingly call our Strategic Assistant® Program Mind Reading 101 because it would help executive assistants understand how entrepreneurs think.

One of the biggest failures of any leader is not being specific enough about what the end results look like. The way I define that is, "What does it look like when it's done and done well?" Getting clarity on that, and communicating it, puts both you and your team on the same page. Then there won't be any surprises— you've been clear on your expectations, and they'll know how to meet your standards.

Dan Sullivan created one of the best tools to help people communicate what they want when he created The Impact Filter™. It's a one-page exercise that helps you get clear on your thinking and then effectively communicate it to others. To go back to the relay race analogy, it's a great way to make the handoff. (For readers who are interested, it's available as a download at *strategic coach.com/go/impactfilter*.)

ZOOMING THROUGH COVID-19

Our business was 100 percent an in-person business. At first, we didn't know what we were going to do. We'd been using Zoom, but only for conversations. A week after lockdown started, an Australian friend of mine, Taki Moore, graciously invited me to attend his online conference. It was supposed to have been held in L.A. but in only five days he converted it to Zoom, ran it from Australia, and did a stellar job. This is where I learned about breakout rooms. I shared it with Babs and our Program Designer, Cathy Davis, and then we had our strategy.

For the first few months, we hosted two-hour Connection Sessions on Zoom for our clients, for free, just to keep them calm, focused, and connected. Then we restarted our all workshops on

Zoom until we could come back in person. Our workshops are very interactive, and we were able to replicate that online and it worked remarkably well. Our team was amazing—they adapted beautifully to working from home and everything else that running workshops virtually entailed.

Dan was a rock—he was our stabilizing force through the changes. Through the pandemic, for 80 to 90 percent of people, a lot stayed the same. But Dan pointed out we simply had to find another way to communicate with people.

Dan insightfully calls Zoom a transportation system, not a communication system. He realized that none of the things that mattered for the company had changed: "My market, my message, the need for it, all those things are still true. I just have to find a different way of getting out there." He even wrote a book called *Zooming Ahead* to encourage our clients to see the value of this new "transportation system."

LEADING IN A PANDEMIC WITH MORALE, MOMENTUM, AND MOTIVATION

There was such a giant need for leadership during the pandemic. People either moved ahead, treaded water, or sank. But Dan did something, not miraculous, but pretty darned close to it as far as leadership is concerned.

On Friday, March 13, 2020, on the flight back to Toronto from Chicago, Babs told him that we wouldn't be holding workshops the following week. So, Dan did what he does when he's confronted with something novel—he reflected on his experience. He thought through when he had experienced other earth-shattering news and handled it well. He thought through how he could use what he'd learned for the current moment. He used this unexpected turn of events to be incredibly innovative and prolific.

Our schedules were blown up because there were no more workshops, so we just focused on creating value. We talked about the *Scary Times Success Manual,* a download that he'd first created after 9/11 to help restore people's confidence and turned it into a twelve-part audio series on our Inside Strategic Coach® podcast, a video series, a whole bunch of new exercises, and a book. Dan and I had a blast. We just tried to give entrepreneurs a safe space where they could think and be creative as opposed to just being freaked the heck out by all the bad news and uncertainty.

Dan realized people would need three things for as long as those hard times lasted. He said, "I just resolved myself to be a source of morale, momentum, and motivation for everybody." And that's who he was. I've never seen a situation where it was more needed and more appreciated. He was a bastion of stability in that chaos, and I had utmost respect for how he handled it.

ENTREPRENEURS NEED TO BE GOOD AT WHO NOT HOW™

Who Not How™ is a transformational business strategy. When we have a new idea or project we want to embark on, instead of asking, "How am I going to do this?" we ask, "Who do I know that knows how to do it?"

When we focus on the Hows, it's de-energizing. If we knew how to do it, we'd already be doing it. If we're doing it ourselves, it means we have to go back to the bottom of the learning curve. Instead, by finding a Who, we have a shortcut.

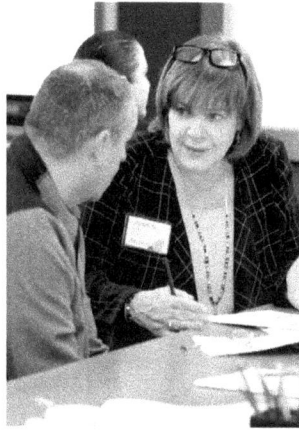

Successful people are usually the ones who focus on surrounding themselves with talented people rather than being the ones who can do everything themselves. And truthfully, there are only a few abilities at which any of us are truly unique.

Lewis Schiff wrote a bunch of great business books, including the well-known *Business Brilliant: Surprising Lessons from the Greatest Self-Made Business Icons*. In another of his books, *The Middle-Class Millionaire*, he and his collaborator, Russ Alan Prince, interviewed several people, from middle-class all the way up to ultra-high net worth, which at that point was 20 to 30 million dollars. They asked the middle-class people how many things they're really, really good at, and the number was five to six. They asked the ultra-high net worth people how many things they're good at, and the average was 1.8. Not even two things!

The ultra-rich know they're not good at a bunch of things, so what do they do? They get the Whos. As entrepreneurs evolve, I believe their goal should be to surround themselves with the best Whos they can find. That way, they can focus on doing the very few activities they love doing and are best at.

Most entrepreneurs are visionaries. They really want to be out there working with clients, writing books, or envisioning the future, not running the company day to day. Frankly, at least for an entrepreneur, most people could run the company better than they could. I love the expression, "If you don't have an assistant, you are one." Entrepreneurs are way too highly paid for some of the tasks that we do, and the quality with which we do them.

SHANNON'S SUPERPOWER

My superpower is coaching, and I shout that from the rooftops. I love listening to people and figuring out the essence of their situation—the heart of their challenge. And then I compassionately communicate practical strategies to align their thinking with where they want to go. I take in what they say, and I don't add to drama. So, I'll be like, "Oh that's interesting. Tell me more about that." Then I'm like, "I can see a couple different ways to approach that."

I coach with love. I'm *for* that person, and I care about them. It's not my situation. I'm not married to it. It might be glaringly obvious to me what needs to happen, but that's not the point. I listen with love, I listen with compassion, and I also listen with intellect. Let's be clear, this is not a therapy session. I help people see things from a multitude of perspectives. I help them get unstuck from what's causing them pain and hopefully help them see another approach.

And with groups, I love co-creating the conversation with the participants. I don't have to have all the answers, just great questions. Together, we create an experience that frees everyone up to be more grounded, clear, and connected to their future. It's an absolute joy.

CHALLENGES TO SHANNON'S LEADERSHIP STYLE

Sometimes, all that joy makes me overly optimistic. I'm not going to say I oversimplify, but I know I sometimes miss the complexities. For example, I didn't think the pandemic was going to last as long as it did. Originally, I thought we'd be back to work in-person in two months—wrong!

And while I'm quite good in emergencies, when something's really jarring or a big deal, I will take a little time to process it and figure out the ramifications. I can tough out the immediate drama, but afterwards I need time to come to terms with it.

I've been very inspired by Kim Scott's book *Radical Candor*, in which she talks about the balance between Caring Personally and Challenging Directly. When you do both, it's Radical Candor. Striking that balance is a growth opportunity for me as I learn how to handle more complex and challenging business and personal situations.

UNIQUELY DAN SULLIVAN

It's tough to thing about all the ways Dan Sullivan is unique as a leader. First of all, he's incredibly self-aware, and he's gotten more so the longer I've known him. He thinks about his thinking, and then he helps other people think about their thinking. I spend a lot of time with him doing our podcast and our quarterly books, and it's like being in the most amazing practical philosophy class. I don't know anyone else who thinks so clearly and practically about life and people.

He's great to work with because he's very clear. He knows what he wants, he doesn't leave anyone guessing, and then he gives people a ton of autonomy to get the project done in the best way they see fit. He is always about Unique Ability® Teamwork.

Dan supports major shifts in the team that supports him, even if it may not be his preference. If that shift will help someone else stay in their Unique Ability®, as opposed to doing something that's stressful for them, he is always a "yes." It helps if the shift is accompanied by an Impact Filter. If someone says, "Dan, this is the intention behind the change." He's like, "Okay." Dan's always committed to being useful and helping other people expand their morale, momentum, and motivation. As someone who works with him, I find it extraordinary.

What you see is what you get with Dan. In our workshop exercises, he writes his own sample copy so people can see what he's thinking about and doing. He's charming and also straightforward. If that works for you, great. If it doesn't, that's fine too. There's something very refreshing about that in the world. He's not trying to please you; he's mostly seeing whether there's a like-mindedness and if he can be useful to you. End of story.

PLANNING FOR SUCCESSION

If entrepreneurs aren't talking about succession because they're scared of it, then that's an issue. I love the fact that Dan and Babs have a financial plan in place for if they're not here. There is a legal plan in place. There is a team in place. They're not leaving the future of the company up in the air if something happens. After all, they travel together.

Dan said, "I want the company to be more profitable ten years from now than from this date." After a client coached him, he amended, "Well, not ten years—the first hundred days." So, a while ago, we went through our First Hundred Days exercise. From that exercise, Dan concluded everyone needed to say what they needed. Babs said a couple of things. From Dan, it was intellectual capital, intellectual capital, intellectual capital. That's when he started the book project. That's why there's a book coming out every quarter. Because I thought, if the worst scenario happens, "I just need a *lot* of Dan. That's what I need. And then I can make it work."

The bottom line for leaders: *Please* don't leave a mess. Do the succession planning even though it's hard. Take care of the people—your family, your team, your clients—for when you're gone so they won't have to deal with the mess when they're mourning you. That's the point.

FUTURE CONVERSATIONS

To be honest, there isn't someone living in the past I'd need to have a conversation with. I don't reference much through talking. I think through reading books, so I get the best of those past people through the words they leave behind.

I'm much more interested in the future. But out of all the future people I'd want to talk to after I'm gone, I would like to talk to my kids the most. I want to see how they're going to turn out, and if they're happy. I don't want to know so much about the things that I could have done differently—I can't change those—but I would like to know what made a difference for them and what didn't.

Shannon Waller is a passionate expert on entrepreneurial teams. With Strategic Coach® since 1991, she's the creator of The Entrepreneurial Team® Program, a parallel program for team members of Coach clients that focuses on fostering a winning Entrepreneurial Attitude in its participants. A key executive and decision-maker at Strategic Coach and a recognized entrepreneurial team expert, Shannon is a sought-after speaker, presenter, and coach.

Shannon is also a Kolbe Certified™ Consultant and the 2015 recipient of the Kolbe Professional Award for individual leadership in building conative excellence. Additionally, she co-authored the bestselling book Unique

Ability® 2.0: Discovery and has written two books about entrepreneurial team success. Her first book, The Team Success Handbook, is a wealth of her distilled teamwork wisdom and includes 12 actionable strategies for working successfully in any entrepreneurial company. Her most recent book, Multiplication By Subtraction, is a comprehensive guide to gracefully letting go of wrong-fit team members.

7

Curiosity Kills
Ron Tite and Church+State

I
T HAS BEEN ONE HELL OF A ROAD TO ENTREPRENEUR-
ial and life success for Ron Tite, going from early childhood
struggles, been raised by his physically disabled mother
after his dad left when he was only a year old.

When you start out in a challenging situation, like Ron, it is
hard to fathom that years later he becomes the founder of an
elite, Toronto-based marketing agency, Church+State, best-selling author of two books, host, and executive producer of the hit
podcast, "The Coup", along with being executive producer &
host of the award-winning comedy show, *Monkey Toast*, and so
much more!

I first met Ron back in 2013. He was speaking at event in Edmonton, and, as he always does, he rocked the audience with his wit

and brilliant insights. Fate brought us back together again, and I had the pleasure to hear him speak again—once at the Canadian Association of Professional Speakers conference in 2016, and again in Edmonton. There is something about Ron that makes you want to hang with him and learn from his creative insights. Ron is an incredibly approachable guy; seriously witty and in my opinion one of the best speakers in Canada.

Back in 2017, I asked Ron to be in my first book, *Remarkable Service*, and was delighted to have Ron accept my offer and contribute to the book.

EARLY BEGINNINGS

Growing up, I shared my childhood with three siblings. My father departed when I was merely a year old, leaving my mother, who is challenged by Spina Bifida, to care for us single-handedly with the aid of social assistance. Despite her mobility limitations and the struggle of walking, she managed to navigate life with resilience. Early on, she underwent the amputation of one leg and contended with a clubfoot on the other. In an instance of a name from a bygone era, her school was starkly titled the "Montreal School for Crippled Children"—a term that, shockingly, didn't seem to disturb her. The name, though jarring to any contemporary ear, was just the mundane reality for her; she mentioned it with no hint of shock or self-pity.

Her ability to work was severely limited, as prolonged standing was not an option for her. Moreover, the school she attended did not exactly champion the future careers of its students; it offered an education only up until grade 10, falling short of preparing them for the professional world.

THE IMPORTANCE OF STORYTELLING

Storytelling has been absolutely critical to my journey through comedy, advertising, and public speaking, all started in my extended Quebecois-Italian family.

In my family, the art of the "bit" was well understood. Within the world of comedy, a "bit" is a crafted piece—a routine honed and performed with precision. Our family gatherings were stages for such bits: stories and jokes meticulously preserved in their original form, passed down and repeated without alteration. Someone would tell the story with all the pauses. All the beats. All the emotions. All the characters. And all the voices that he had used every time before. Over time, the story became perfected much in the same way a comedian perfects a bit on the road. Everyone in the room knew exactly how the story was going to end but they still reacted with the laughter they expressed the first time they heard it. They were an attentive and supportive audience. And when it was their turn to tell their story, they stepped to the metaphorical mic in the middle of the room and delivered.

This was the essence of a "bit," and from a really young age, I was an eyewitness to this tradition. It was more than storytelling—it was a summons to the stage, an invitation to captivate and entertain.

DISCOVERING MY DRIVE

When I was seven, we got a stepdad who was a verbally abusive alcoholic. Fun times. He just passed away. It was a weird upbringing of huge contrasts—a loud and angry environment that was balanced by my mom, who was an incredible, joyful, fun, and positive person who—by all accounts—should not have been.

I think I just continually thought, "It's got to be better than this, right?"

The first time I saw the movie Meatballs, I went to my mom and asked, "What is camp?" She said, "People go to a place and play baseball and other sports." I said, "Oh, I'd like to try that." But in my brain, I was thinking, "I want to get the hell out of here. I want to go and experience something new." But, of course, we couldn't afford to send me. When I hit 17, I found out I could go work at a camp as a counselor, so I applied to the Ontario Camping Association, got aligned with a camp, got interviewed, and finally got to go to Camp Kennebec. I didn't know it, but Kennebec was predominantly Jewish—not religiously Jewish, just mostly people from Montreal who just happened to be Jewish. Suddenly, and without warning, I was introduced to a world where people had cultural *and* socio-economic perspectives that were really, really different than mine. That was eye-opening. And more rewarding than I could have ever imagined.

AN ACCIDENTAL EDUCATION

I accidentally went to Queen's University in Kingston, Ontario. The only reason I went there was that teaching was the only non-blue-collar career to which I had been exposed. I respected my wrestling coach, who had gone to Queen's and studied Phys-ed. So, I decided I'd do that, too.

Once there, I met all these interesting people from a wide variety of backgrounds, with parents who had all these interesting careers. I quickly realized, "Oh God, I don't want to be a teacher." It's a wonderful career, and I respect teachers, but I simply realized it wasn't exactly a calling for me. I just knew that there were other experiences that I didn't know about.

I read a book called *The Imaginary Girlfriend*, an autobiography by John Irving. John was a competitive amateur wrestler, as was I, so I always related to him. In this book, Irving wrote about discovering his love of writing while he was also wrestling in college. His love of writing became so strong that he would lie to his coach and say, "I can't go to the meet because I'm going to see my girlfriend." In reality, his girlfriend was his writing.

He showed me how someone could have a passion for something. I didn't know you could be passionate about something and pursue it. I thought you worked all day, watched TV, and then went to bed and repeated it the next day.

With that, I realized I didn't have to do Phys Ed—that I could do whatever brought me great joy. I could write. I could paint. I could do tax accounting. Whatever. I just needed to find my own version of an imaginary girlfriend.

Flash ahead 20 years later. My second book, *Think Do Say*, was about to be published. I was having dinner with Jesse Finkelstein, my publisher from Page Two, and sitting beside me...was John Irving. As he was leaving, I stopped him and said, "Look, I know other people probably come up to you and talk about *Garp* and *Cider House Rules* and *Owen Meany* and everything else, but I need to tell you that *Imaginary Girlfriend* changed my life."...

I went on to tell him about my life as a wrestler, my life as a writer, and introduced him to Jesse. He was lovely. He was gracious. And I still can't believe it happened.

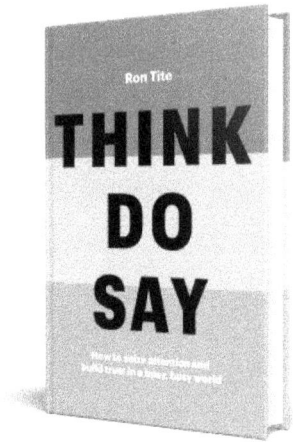

TAKING THE LEAP

After I left camp, I worked in the Queen's business school leading health and fitness sessions that were part of a series of executive development programs. They offered to bring me on full-time as Program Manager for the National Executive MBA Program. It was headed by Gordon Cassidy. Oddly, he was both a professor of statistics and probably the best entrepreneur I've ever worked with. This was the guy who said, "We're going to link 11 cities across the country through video conferencing, and we're going to teach an MBA program from one of the best schools in the country." Developing that program was a career-defining moment because nobody had done this before. And to do it within academia? Within the ivory towers of Queen's? It was a start-up in an environment that was not built for start-ups. When I asked Gordon why he would want a Phys-Ed grad instead of a BComm, he said, "Only rocket science is rocket science. Look, here's why I want you. Number one, you went to Queen's, so you're clearly bright. Secondly, you have grown up with sports and athletics, and you understand the very nature of teams and an individual's contribution to team effort. You get that. Thirdly, you're social, and people relate to you, and you're good to hang out with. And lastly, you're competitive, and you understand what it takes to compete and win. Those are far more important skills than learning accounting."

Here's a funny thing. Of the six program managers in the Queen's School of Business, running the most innovative executive MBA programs in the world, four of the six were Phys-Ed grads. I did that for three years, and then a web company, Affinity Edge, asked me to join them. This was 1996. I didn't really understand the web. But nobody understood it because it was so new. Here's an interesting metaphor that helps illustrate this: I never skied growing up. So I never skied as an adult simply because I didn't want to be the guy who had never skied. But then snowboarding was created, and nobody knew how to snowboard. So, I started snowboarding. I got ahead of the curve by learning the new thing instead of beating myself up about not knowing the old thing. That's the perfect time to learn it. Affinity Edge was partners with an ad agency. One day, I told a story to somebody who worked for the ad agency. It was a funny story. She went to the two owners of the agency and said, "That guy's funny." Affinity Edge was going through some challenges. The owner is still a great friend, Mike Tobias, and I just offered to leave. One of the partners in the ad agency approached me.

Him: You ever think about a career in advertising?
Me: Nope.
Him: Ok. You'll be an account guy. Being an account guy is basically making a list and checking it off. You're smart enough to know what goes on the list and you're ambitious enough to do the things so that you can check them off.
Me: Okaaaaaayyyyy...
Him: You're an account supervisor. We'll pay you whatever they were paying you.

I was curious about it, so I pursued it. Curiosity is also what got me into stand-up. I didn't start thinking, "I want to be a comedian in a stadium performing to 40,000 people." I just wanted the experience of doing stand-up so I could figure out the method to the madness. So I went to my good friend, Steve Patterson, who's now the host of The Debaters on CBC.

> *Me*: I know I want to do stand-up. I've always loved the craft. What do I do?
>
> *Steve*: Go to Yuk Yuk's and go on open mic night. It's Monday night. You sign up, you get five minutes on stage. You just keep doing that every week, and if they like you, they'll bring you back for a Tuesday where you get to do seven minutes.

I first went to just check it out and watch, and it was the biggest shit show I've ever seen in my life. It was horrible. It was horrible comedy. It was demeaning to the people who were doing it.

Before I even started, I knew I was already better than every single person who went up on stage. It wasn't about being cocky. It was about being serious about the pursuit. And I did not want to be associated with that type of comedy.

I went back to Steve.

> *Me*: I'm not doing that. What else can I do?
>
> *Steve*: The only other thing you can do is get to know a producer who's producing a live show and convince them to give you five minutes, even though you've never done it before.
>
> *Me*: Why don't I just *become* a producer? Why don't I just produce my own show and do what I want?

And that's how it's done, really: You book a room. You announce a show. And just do it. I simply wanted to do it my own way. It was just one night, and I didn't care if it succeeded or failed.

So just like that, I produced my own show, made myself the headliner, and the very first time I ever did stand-up comedy, I did a 45-minute headlining set.

THE COMEDY EQUATION

A key part of comedy is finding and uncovering the pain and exploring how to deal with it in a humourous way. Interestingly, that process is the exact same thing that entrepreneurs do. They find the customer's pain and explore how to solve that problem. Creatively, then they can use humour to illuminate the problem or talk about the solution, you just explore the problem in a really humourous way.

THE MOMENT OF CHANGE

It was from the most powerful moment I've ever had on stage.

I was curious about how I could take my stand-up material and turn it into a play form. This director said, "Well, then you need to expose the pain. Emotion is the thread through all the funny, but you need to expose the pain behind the comedy to reveal the emotions of the comedy. You don't ever talk about the pain in your comedy. You just add the funny part. Expose the pain. Reveal the emotions. *That's* a play."

So, I did that. I wrote this play, *The Canadian Baby Bonus*. Near the end of the play, the character says, "So hey. Be careful." The "be careful" is a callback to something earlier in the play, and it's rather poignant, and it's kind of the meaning of the play. So, I'm performing it at the Edmonton Fringe Festival. Full house. Near the end, I say, "So hey," and the room is silent. And all I hear in the front row...is one woman gasp—it was the slightest little inhale of air that cut through the silence of the room, and it's the most powerful moment I've ever had on stage.

It was powerful because I knew that I had her completely in the palm of my hand. I knew that I could take her wherever I wanted to take her. I realized in that moment what the true power of comedy was and that very few people even use the power. That it's not about the punchline. It's about what follows the punchline. You can set a crowd up with funny, but once you have them, you can deliver something really important. Or really emotional. Or really strategic. If you just end at the punchline, it's empty calories. But if you actually take it a step deeper and make people think about what the comedy set up...that's really powerful.

At that moment, I knew I wanted more. I thought, "How do I get more of *that* feeling? How can I be more satisfied by the silence that follows the laugh than the laugh itself?"

FROM COMEDY TO BUSINESS

People don't buy a comedian who knows about business. They just don't. So that was the first major pivot I had to make: I went from being "a comedian who knows about business" to "a funny business guy". Same product. Different positioning.

That pivot changed everything. It changed the focus from comedy to speaking. It changed the focus from using speaking as a business development tool to advertising. It got me more credibility with advertising because, up to that point, I was just the funny guy. And then that grew to the point that I was now executive creative director at a multinational agency. Eventually, as all these interests and pursuits came together, I needed to control my own destiny. And the only way to do that was to start my own thing.

That's when I started The Tite Group. Initially, I thought it needed to be called The Tite Group because Ron Tite, "The Speaker," needed to be associated with the agency, "The Tite Group". Then my friend Neil Pasricha, who wrote *The Book of Awesome*, said, "Oh, this is a whole agency? I thought the Tite Group was just you, because speakers who have companies with their personal name in the corporate title are usually operating them out of their garage. You need to change that."

Think about it—if X5 was called "Mack Development and Coaching", people would think it was just you, Mike Mack, on your own. It was a great point from Neil, and we rebranded.

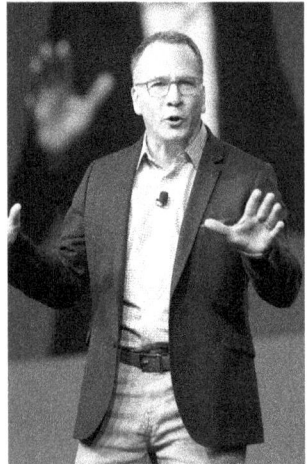

The brief to the team was simple: *I want a new name. I want less Tite, more Group. This cannot be about Ron. It's got to be about the agency as a whole.*

Once I did that, it was freeing. Then the agency really took off.

ENTREPRENEURSHIP: THE GOOD, THE BAD, AND THE UGLY

The great part about entrepreneurship is that you can do whatever you want. It's completely freeing and empowering. Every decision is totally up to you. You can go with your gut.

But the challenge of that is also that *you can do whatever you want*. Many entrepreneurs are driven by passion and ideas, but it takes a big person to realize that just because you start your own thing, maybe you're not the best person to *run* your own thing.

If you really want the business to grow, in most cases entrepreneurs need great partners who can take the business from concept car to assembly line—which is where you actually make money.

If you want to scale the business:

- That means process.
- That means rules.
- That means responsibilities.
- That means personal accountability.
- That means a fine eye on the finances.

All those things I have neither the talent nor the desire nor the passion to get involved with. I just don't. It's not that I don't care; I know how important they are. I just get no joy out of looking at a spreadsheet, and I add zero value. I get no great joy out of reinforcing process even though I know it's fundamentally critical to the success of the business.

Right from the beginning, I knew I'd rather own 25% of 5x then 100% of x.

When you start as an entrepreneur, you think you need to have all the answers. You need to be the CEO. You need to be the one. *No, you don't.* That's like saying if you're a stand-up comedian, you need to stand there with a mic and talk about airplanes. No. It's your stage, it's your mic. You can do whatever the hell you want. The only thing that matters is that it's a good show.

I think it takes a big personality and a big ego to put yourself out there and take risks; you have to have an incredible faith in your abilities. But it takes true confidence to understand where your strengths and weaknesses are and how you need to be complemented—complemented by people who have *different* skills and abilities.

DEFINING SUCCESS

I definitely don't define success as money. And that's not to say I don't charge what I think I'm worth and what the market says I can charge—and I want to be paid fairly. But for me, it's never been about the pursuit of money, because if you just pursue money, you'll never have enough.

For me, it really is just about happiness and fulfillment. I often say: the only KPI is happiness.

That said, if you don't pursue some turbulent times, if you never look to be challenged, you'll never have the escalated joys of overcoming challenges and barriers.

On the family side, it's the same thing.

Some people say, "It's only about my family," and they sacrifice everything else for the love of the family. That's not me.

I want my kids to pursue careers they get great fulfillment from, that they succeed in, and that they're happy in. It's my job to show them what that looks like. I need to show them somebody who is engaged and passionate about their life beyond the home. At the same time, they also need to see someone who is committed to family and who finds great joy in family – not out of default or obligation, but out of pure joy. I need to show them that I absolutely love them and love spending time with them.

I remember when we were about to have our first child. Given the shitty dad and stepdad that I'd had, I told my wife, "I just want to be a good dad. That's all I want to be for them. I just want to be a good dad."

A few months ago, I was with Max, our oldest. I kiss my kids 400 times a day; I'm always hugging and kissing them. Max asked me, "Why do you always kiss me?!" I told him, "You know, my Daddy never kissed me. So I always want to show you that I love you."

I thought nothing of it. Two days later, the whole family was in the car, stopped at a traffic light. I suddenly heard Max's little inquisitive voice from the back seat: "Daddy, why didn't your daddy kiss you?"

He had thought about it for two days. It had clearly both shook him and perplexed him.

I thought it may have been troubling for him, so I just downplayed it. "Oh, my daddy was always away, and I never got to see him. Daddies didn't really kiss their kids back then." He was four. It was too complex a thing. He'll find out later.

My biggest concern with my kids isn't, "Are they going to have food on their plate?" It's "Do they have it too easy? Are they going to appreciate success the way I appreciate it?"

ADVICE FOR ASPIRING ENTREPRENEURS

Build out the team. As an entrepreneur, you can't do everything all the time; you need people to complement your skills. You can't scale a person. How are you building a team that can bring your idea to market and scale your idea?

THE ROAD AHEAD

It's the idea that CX (customer experience) isn't possible without EX (employee experience). I think there's a tighter relationship between marketing and HR that needs to happen. If we know that customer experience is really important and we also know that people deliver that customer experience, then how does an agency who deals with external messaging go in and train people to deliver that customer experience?

That's something that agencies have never done before. It's been outside their bailiwick. It's something I want to pursue because I think that gives us a competitive advantage and a unique place in the market.

FUNDAMENTALS OF LEADERSHIP AND ENTREPRENEURSHIP

Gordon Cassidy said, "Only rocket science is rocket science". When you look at what's happening out there in the market, entire categories are being overthrown and taken out by people who have no previous experience in that category. It's that fresh perspective. Not only do you not have to have experience, in some cases, that experience becomes baggage and a barrier to true growth.

Named one of the "Top 10 Creative Canadians" by Marketing Magazine, bestselling author, speaker, producer, and entrepreneur Ron Tite blurs the lines between art and commerce. He's an award-winning advertising writer and creative director for some of the world's most respected brands including Air France, Fidelity, Google, Johnson & Johnson, Intel, Microsoft, Volvo and many others.

He is founder of Church+State, host and executive producer of the hit podcast The Coup, and publisher of *This is That Travel Guide to Canada*, a best-selling and award-winning satirical book. He has written for television. Penned a children's book. Wrote, produced, and performed a hit play. Created a branded art gallery. And was executive producer & host of the award-winning comedy show, *Monkey Toast*.

CHURCH +STATE

In demand as a speaker all over the world, Ron speaks to leading organizations about leadership, disruption, growth, and creativity. Ron's first book, *Everyone's an Artist—Or At Least They Should Be* (co-written by Scott Kavanagh and Christopher Novais), was published by HarperCollins in 2016. His most recent book, *Think Do Say: How to Seize Attention and Build Trust in a Busy, Busy World*, came out in October of 2019.

8

Keep your Eye on the Sky

Richard Hansen and Sky Eye Measurement

RICHARD HANSEN IS THE PRESIDENT & CEO OF Sky Eye Measurement, founded in Valleyview, Alberta in 2005 to serve the upstream Oil and Gas Market. Today, Sky Eye provides solutions and services for some of the world's largest producers across North America.

Richard guides Sky Eye's high-level operations and manages Sky Eye's growth and strategy. Known for his tireless entrepreneurial drive, Richard received the esteemed Ernst and Young Entrepreneur of the Year award for Energy Services (Prairies) in 2019.

Sky Eye's vibrant culture is a testament to Richard's goal to make Sky Eye "the best place you've ever worked." With decades of energy experience, Richard is an energetic and inspiring leader who has created a truly unique and dynamic environment in Sky Eye.

I was introduced to Richard Hansen in early 2021 by a friend and business connection, Leanne Burrows, who was the Director, Communications and Marketing at Sky Eye Measurement. Leanne and I worked on a project a few years early with a former company.

When I first connected with Richard via a Zoom call, we had an instant connection. I admired his energy and the passion he showed in the business and how he operated as an entrepreneur.

Soon after that, I supported Richard and his team in a coaching and consulting capacity. It wasn't until June 2021 (six months later) that Richard and I met in person, sitting on my patio and enjoying a beer with a few other clients and fellow CEOs.

THE JOURNEY BEGINS

At the beginning of my career, like most people, I wanted a stable job that paid well and offered a rewarding career path. I graduated from the Power Engineering program at the Northern Alberta Institute of Technology (NAIT) in Edmonton back in 1990. Right after graduation, I started working at Gulf Canada in a production operation role at the Meekwap field. During my five years there, I took the opportunity to apprentice in instrumentation, which led me into the trade.

I haven't been with many companies, but I've moved around quite a bit for work. Getting to work in different places with new teams and equipment has been a huge boost to my adaptability and continuous learning.

Early on, I was keen on the idea of working abroad. I used to think, "If I don't end up going overseas, the one place I'd really like to work is in the Red Deer and Sylvan Lake area of Central Alberta." I just loved it there. In 1997, I got the chance to make that move. I settled in Red Deer and stayed put until I started Sky Eye in 2005. By that time, I had completed my journeyman instrumentation certification and gained experience working in both a gas plant and in the oil and gas field.

My time with Gulf Canada came to a close when it was acquired by the American company Conoco, which later merged with Phillips to become ConocoPhillips. I spent 16 years with the company, which gave me a solid foundation and invaluable experience to draw upon when I shifted my focus to entrepreneurship.

DRIVEN TO BE DIFFERENT

Around 2000, shortly after I met my wife, Jenn, I felt a drive to do something different and unique and try something new. My current business partner Allen Caron (Chum) was also a big inspiration. He had started a business in 1994 at the age of 22, and I remember thinking he was crazy for doing it because there was just so much risk back in the early nineties.

Chum became very successful with his business. We have been lifelong friends; our families even farmed together. From the age of 12 we'd spent summers working together in the field making hay. To this day we still enjoy working together and have amazing rapport.

My time at ConocoPhillips doing SCADA (Supervisory Control and Data Acquisition) automation was at the prime of my life. I felt as though I had gained enough experience to really feel confident in what I was doing and was ready to take the next step.

You can start a business at any time. It all depends on your level of maturity and what kind of confidence you have.

AN EXPERIENCED PARTNER

It's amazing how much confidence you can have when your partner is already a successful business owner. I was able to learn how to really set up a business for success from the help of Al and his parents, Gus and Louise Caron. They played a key factor at the beginning Sky Eye.

During my time at ConocoPhillips, third party companies required our SCADA systems for gas and liquid measurement of their wells to tie into the main facility. Part of my job was to provide customers with a way to implement the SCADA systems for these companies. Typically, it sounded like, "We could do it for you or you can buy it yourself, but it's going to be $32,000."

AN IDEA IS BORN

The idea sparked when a customer preferred to rent our equipment rather than buy it, unsure about the lifespan of their gas well. At the time, my company didn't offer rentals.

So, I called Chum and asked if he knew anyone who rented out this kind of gear. He hadn't, but promised to look into it. Later, he reported back with no leads and asked if I saw a real demand for it. Indeed, a few companies had inquired about renting SCADA measurement equipment.

A year on, over beers in Calgary, Chum and I were hashing out the rental idea when an industry veteran chimed in, "Rentals are a smart move for companies." That comment solidified our belief in the need and boosted our confidence to start Sky Eye.

As Chum and I delved deeper, we saw the need to offer not just measurement, but also automation that could bump up production. We envisioned a service that provided precise measurements and boosted the well's profitability.

Our initial brainstorming sessions were casual, just bouncing ideas off each other on napkins. Chum then brought in Boyd Viker and Terry Hannas, his tech experts, to refine the product design and strategy. By October 2005, we had a clear plan: automate the gear,

ensure precise measurement, add SCADA and internet connectivity, all in a solar-powered setup easy to haul on a trailer. The key was to enable data access for multiple customers through a secure login. (Richard in the early days)

We partnered with a company for hosting our equipment data securely online. Combining our expertise in field measurement and automation, we crafted these portable units and started renting them out, mainly to Chum's contacts. It was a side project at first, worked on over weekends and free time, until I decided to leave my job at ConocoPhillips and fully commit to this new venture.

BUSINESS EVOLVING ALONGSIDE LIFE

In 2006 I lived in Sylvan Lake, Alberta, and we just had our second child, Emma, who was born in 2005. Our first daughter, Kayla was 3 years old, and Emma was less than a year old when we decided I needed to move to Valleyview if the company was going to be successful. Chum had too much on his plate with his own company, I had the business plan created and it was time to do the transition and become active in the business.

With this transition to start my own company, I had the full support and backing of my wife. I knew I was ready. I'd spent 16 years with one company, we had just recently been married in 2001, and now we were ready for the next phase in life. I told myself, "Well, if I'm going to try this now, I'm only 34 and if it fails, I can still recover."

Not that I ever, ever anticipated it would fail, but of course you must have that honest open conversation with yourself, right?

Thankfully, my wife had a great full-time job, and she made more money than I did. So that was a good support mechanism and helped with the confidence of starting a business because our original investment was $20,000. And I remember saying to Chum, "Well, I'm going to have to borrow $10,000." And he said, "You don't have $20,000 to invest in a business right now?" Then I said, "No, we just bought a house, and I have to borrow $10,000." He said, "Well, all the more reason you better get into business."

EARLY CHALLENGES

We found ourselves needing to borrow another $80,000. Back then, personal guarantees were a must since we didn't have collateral or assets. Having a business partner like Chum was beneficial, as he was already well-established, but we still had to risk everything at the start. You need the capital to build equipment, and then the real challenge begins: securing work to generate income. Introducing our concept of renting out SCADA measurement equipment was tough; clients were skeptical.

In the early stages, we had to be generous. We offered what we called a "try-before-you-buy-or-rent" deal. Our pitch was simple: cover our time to set up, and use the equipment for a couple of weeks or a month, free of charge. If it didn't meet their needs, we'd take it back at no extra cost. This approach proved the worth of our equipment and demonstrated how we could help clients improve their profits.

We started with basic services like accurate EFM (electronic flow measurement) checks, well monitoring, and production optimization controls. We even installed timers so operators could remotely adjust settings from home or the office. Once online, they could see their data, chart progress, and notice incremental production increases.

Typically, we'd run our equipment alongside theirs for a short period to establish a performance baseline. After a week or two, we'd initiate the automation for remote operation. It wasn't long before the benefits became clear, as companies could easily see the value in the incremental improvements we provided.

UNIQUE BUSINESS FACTORS

Sky Eye gives you the ability to remotely monitor your wells and then optimize them allowing you to remotely see what was going on with your well. At the time, we had a combination of cell and satellite services; not a lot of companies were offering satellite communication services. So, if you didn't have cell service, it didn't matter. We were able to retrieve your data remotely. This information was accessible on the internet and automated at your home or office, and this was a big deal in 2005 – 2006.

The real jewel was the level of service that we provided; we would give clients the option to try our product at no cost. It was a combination of technical and commercial excellence that accelerated the growth of Sky Eye mostly by referrals.

Another thing that was just starting to take off was incorporating water cut measurement, not just gas, but a water cut measurement device. As we continued to grow and innovate our product line another added value to the customer was the addition of electronic water cut measurement. This type of measurement was a newer technology that was not fully trusted by our customers. Completing a manual sample verification in our sample cut procedures allowed us to prove the accuracy of the meter. We built up to 15 portable units that were all rented.

In the summer of 2008, things couldn't have been better. Fast forward to the fall of 2008 and the global financial collapse, in which the price of oil hit around $40 a barrel. Companies we worked for went into heavy cost reduction. That was our first taste of adversity, the first downturn.

LIVING ON THE EDGE

During the economic downturn in January 2009, our company was down to just four people. Through the previous autumn, our rental units began to return one by one. By the end of January, we had only four or five units out in the field. Calls came in one after the other: "We're done with this unit. Please pick it up. We can't pay for it anymore." Suddenly, all our equipment was back, and our revenue had dried up.

The silver lining was that we had managed to pay off our debt by the second year and had been growing through cash flow. We didn't have any outstanding debts, which was a relief. The company had to scale back to just Chum and me. I was flying solo for any new work while Chum's other business ventures were still thriving. Sky Eye, however, was in a lull. I kept asking myself, "Is this how it all ends? How do we pull through this?"

We were on the brink of losing it all. With no work, sustaining a business seemed impossible. I had to shake off the defeatist attitude. I hadn't left a solid job and moved my family for it all to come to nothing. The pressure was immense.

Chum, ever the optimist and visionary, helped me see things differently. He always had a way of finding the upside, saying, "Don't stress about it. Business is like baseball; you won't always get the pitch you want. You might strike out sometimes, but then, out of nowhere, you'll hit a home run. The key is to stay in the game, to be ready at the plate."

Being "at the plate" was his metaphor for staying in business. You can't score if you're not in the game, and you certainly can't hit a home run if you're not up to bat. That's the mindset we clung to—staying present, ready for our next opportunity, no matter how tough things got.

Jobs slowly began to return by the spring of 2009. We landed our first gig in a while, a sparse but promising liquid measurement project with Talisman. Chum and I got to work, assembling all the equipment in about a week. When they placed the order, they needed it installed ASAP. "How soon can you deliver?" they asked. "Give us a week," I told them. And just like that, installation was scheduled for Good Friday.

That year, my children were young, and I spent the entire Easter weekend working, missing Easter morning with them. I remember telling my wife, Jenn, "I'll be gone before the kids are up, but I'll be back for dinner." It was a bittersweet moment, knowing these special mornings with your little ones are few. But the gratitude for having work again was overwhelming.

A STEADY RECOVERY

After securing the job with Talisman, work gradually began to increase. By 2010, we had earned a solid reputation and business was picking up. Up until then, we hadn't sold any of our rental equipment; we were strictly a rental business. Customers had asked to purchase our equipment, appreciating its quality and ease of use. I was hesitant, though, as it was my own proprietary design, and I wasn't keen on selling it.

Despite turning down several offers, I realized that if we didn't sell, our customers would simply find someone else who would. So, we made the decision to start selling our older rental equipment at a discount. This could be parts or even the whole unit, which marked our transition from purely rentals to a combination of sales and rentals.

Entering the sales market was an eye-opener. It expanded our customer base significantly since not everyone is interested in renting. Selling to customers turned out to be an incredible move, broadening our reach far beyond what I had initially imagined as a rental-only outfit.

MAXIMIZING THE MARKET

Selling equipment brought its own rhythm, with build cycles that could stretch to four weeks for certain items. We expanded our offerings to include truck offload skids, transloaders, and various measurement solutions. By 2011, business was booming, enabling us to hire more staff, including Kevin Quilichini, who would become our VP of Operations and Sales, and Nicole Ferguson, our future Administrative Manager. Come 2012, Sky Eye was surging ahead; we grew to around 10 employees and opened a new shop in South Edmonton. Diving into the crude oil transloader market, we broadened our reach across Western Canada, offering rental solutions that bridged the gap for customers while we tailored equipment for their specific needs.

The years 2012 and 2013 were particularly vibrant, allowing us to build a strong core team. This shift enabled me to step back from the technical side and focus on steering our company's vision and growth. Empowering our staff to contribute to product innovation was crucial during this phase. In three years, we sold 74 units, drawing in new customers and entering fresh markets, including the refined fuel sector.

In 2014, we upgraded from a 3,500 square foot workshop to a 12,000 square foot facility in Acheson, just west of Edmonton. However, the industry took a hard hit with a steep decline in oil prices, causing a drop in sales. Despite this, we retained our core team of 20 and had enough backlog work to sustain us through 2015. But 2016 brought the real downturn.

Our saving grace came from diversifying into refined fuel and LPG units. Sales to a client in Brownsville, Texas not only got us through but also paved our way into the USA and Mexico. By 2017 and 2018, these regions became critical to our growth, accounting for half our revenue. The Canadian market rebounded in the summer of 2018, leading to a momentous opportunity when John Forchuk, our VP of Business Development, announced a chance to build 25 units in four weeks, with the first five needed in just one week.

Our team rose to the challenge, completing the order for BP in the Permian Basin, Texas. This contract was a game-changer, a true home run that propelled us to new levels of capability and achievement.

ENTREPRENEUR OF THE YEAR

I got the call from Matthew Peddie at EY because he would drive by our shop, and he phones me. And he says, "This is Matthew with Ernst & Young. And I just want a minute to chat about your business if you have time." I said, "Sure, sure. It's all good." And he goes, "I just want to learn a little bit more." He goes, "You're in the energy services business." I said, "Yeah. That's our thing." He goes, "How are you so busy every time I drive by your shop? I see a lot of other people not that busy."

So, then I kind of give him a precursor of what we do and how we do it and our involvement into the US and Mexico. Then Matthew and two other accountants visited the shop and did a complete site tour. We spent about two hours with them, and they asked several questions, and after the interview, they're like, "Would you be okay with us nominating you for Entrepreneur of the Year? Because we love this story."

In October of 2019, I won Entrepreneur of the Year for Energy Services in the Prairie division. This was very unexpected and a huge honor. This award really helped establish the confidence within our team to deliver, build, and execute to grow our company to the next level. Then from there the award nominations started coming in, we had a detailed business strategy. Yet we really didn't have an established sales team. With only John Forchuk, Grace Corey, and me in business development, and our technical team handling quotations, all the sales were driven by word of mouth, client referrals, and a handful of conferences.

After I won Entrepreneur of the Year, I was invited to the Ernst & Young Growth Forum in Palm Springs in November. That really opened my eyes and inspired me just listening to other entrepreneurs and their stories and what they did.

They're all the same.

- There are always similarities.
- They're facing adversity.
- There's huge amount of risk at any moment.
- Things can go south fast if you don't watch your bottom line.
- What really matters the most is your perseverance and your mindset.
- You must have a clear mind and understand that better days are out there.
- Take care of your people and they will take care of business.

Listening to the stories of others' experiences sparked inspiration in me. While sharing a beer, I found myself at a crossroads discussing our new shop and my ambition for growth. "What do you envision?" he asked. "A $50 million or a $100 million company?" His own business, started from scratch, was now valued at a quarter of a billion. "It boils down to the risks you're willing to take," he advised. I realized I wanted to match the pace of my team and aim high.

He emphasized the necessity of commitment: "Choose your path and pursue it wholeheartedly." Indeed, entrepreneurship demands more than full attention; it requires an unwavering 110 percent dedication. Half-hearted efforts rarely lead to success. Growth often means gambling everything on your vision.

When our company experienced rapid growth in late 2019, time was too short to construct a new facility. We considered buying or leasing, and soon, a 50,000 square foot space became available. It was ambitious—twice what we needed—but it pointed us in the right direction. After several restless nights, I made the decision: we could handle it. With that, we went "all in" and bought the building, moving in by January. Looking back at January 2020, I believed it was the best decision ever made.

Our team thrived in the safety and space of the new environment, a stark contrast to the cramped and hazardous conditions of our previous location. With over a hundred employees, our operations were smooth and efficient. But just as we hit our stride, feeling unstoppable, we were faced with a global pandemic.

PREPARING FOR THE UNSEEN

Life and business are unpredictable—just when you think you've reached the peak, be ready for a challenge. We faced such a challenge head-on when the pandemic hit, halting business worldwide. As everything came to a standstill, and work retracted, we saw significant contracts delayed or cancelled. Adapting to these circumstances was crucial as we navigated maintaining a vast space and managing costs.

Adversity is inevitable; what matters is your response. Our team embraced the necessary changes, and this collective resilience is paying off. We weathered the initial storm, but 2021 tested us more severely, much like the difficulties we experienced in 2015 and 2016. Back then, a backlog of work provided some momentum, but the real impact was felt in the second year without a quick recovery. Despite the hardships of 2021, we've seen a strong comeback.

It feels good. It's starting to feel half normal like how things were prior to moving into this building before the pandemic slapped our business in the face!

MY LEADERSHIP SUPERPOWER

My superpower is probably putting together great teams and bringing together great people. I believe it's not about me and it's important to surround yourself with smart, hardworking individuals. Even as a leader you aspire to be like them, and we all have something to teach each other.

YOU'RE NOT BORN AN ENTREPRENEUR

You're not born an entrepreneur; I sure wasn't. My parents raised us to be successful and to work hard with integrity and intention. Success is dependent on who you surround yourself with. Who do you go to for advice? Who is there that's going to support you and help you with your ideas, in a collaborative way where they create awareness of your blind spots and your faults?

FUTURE BUSINESS GOALS

In the next three years I'd like to have a strong presence in the US strategically. That's huge. I want to be outside of North America. I want to be global. I want to have our equipment in Europe, South America. Everybody moves fuel throughout the world, and everybody can take advantage of our technology and our equipment. Right now, we're focused on the North American market. Ultimately global expansion with a team where everybody's happy, challenged, rewarded, and always smiling.

I get inspired by our people.

What gets me up in the morning and brings me to work is great people. I just love the collaboration and camaraderie. Expanding the business, is exciting, but I love the growth of the people. When you look at our leadership group, and you look at how many people in our management and leadership have been with us since we became significant during the first four or five years before the 2008 downturn, we came a long way from the one-man band trying to find our way in the world.

WISDOM FOR YOUNG ENTREPRENEURS

Diligence is key—always strive to be the most hardworking person in the room. Businesses flourish not on their own but through persistent effort. Resilience is essential; downturns and failures are inevitable, but they guarantee growth. Stay adaptable, innovate, and keep your goals in sight. It's your passion that will fuel you, the force that propels you to rise each day with purpose.

Building a business means cultivating a stellar team. As an entrepreneur, your vision sets the course, but a dedicated team brings it to life. They're the backbone of your enterprise, caring for your business and clients. The importance of this cannot be overstated. Aim for unparalleled customer service, a hallmark of your brand. As you've often reminded me, Mike, leave nothing to chance!

Richard Hansen is the president and co-founder of Sky Eye Measurement, a measurement solutions company in Alberta, Canada, with a substantial presence across North America. Richard founded Sky Eye Measurement in 2005. Today, Sky Eye Measurement is known as a "Global Leader in Energy Transfer Solutions" and has offices in Acheson, Calgary, Monterrey and Houston. Sky Eye's rapidly growing team of 135 comprises Engineers, Designers, Journeyman Pipefitters, Welders, Electricians, Automation Technicians, Site Service Personnel, and more.

Richard and Sky Eye have been the recipients of prestigious awards like the EY Entrepreneur of the Year (2019), Business in Edmonton's Business Leaders (2018), and Alberta Chamber of Commerce Global Growth Award Finalist (2020). The ABA Medium Business of the Year Award (2022) and the ABA Innovation Award (2023).

9

Mentorship Matters

Koleya Karringten and Absolute Combustion

W HEN YOU THINK OF A RESILIENCE AND PER-
sistence, think of our next leader, Koleya Karringten. She is one impressive entrepreneur!

Based in Calgary, Alberta, Koleya is a proud technology entrepreneur, advocate, and leader. She has a unique perspective on
the challenges and opportunities of product commercialization,
ecosystem building, and fostering inclusion in the technology
industry.

As the co-founder and CEO of Absolute Combustion, she
has spent over a decade successfully designing and developing

ground-breaking cleantech solutions for multiple industry sectors, including aerospace and oil and gas. She is a driving force in Canada's blockchain technology industry as the executive director of the Canadian Blockchain Consortium (CBC) and co-founder and board member of the Canadian Blockchain Association for Women (CBAW).

In her leadership role at the CBC, she merged her passions for technology and social good to bring together blockchain companies, corporate leaders, and the government to build the country's largest blockchain ecosystem organization. An influential public speaker, writer, and community volunteer, Koleya strongly believes that uniting diverse voices behind a common goal is the path to creating a fairer, more sustainable, and prosperous nation.

Get ready to learn Koleya's journey as an entrepreneur—the lessons learned from her mentors, as well as her tragic hardships along the way.

A FATHER'S INFLUENCE

Growing up in Vancouver, Canada, my journey toward entrepreneurship, advocacy, and leadership in technology innovation began at a young age. I was raised in a family where business, inventiveness, critical thinking, and finance were imbedded in the fabric of daily life and my natural curiosity and creativity was fostered in a very supportive home environment. The largest influence in my life was my father, Darsell Karringten, a gifted entrepreneur and inventor who identified my talents early on. He sought to expose me to a wider world of ideas and experiences, including taking me to see world-renowned business speaker, Jim Rohn, at just eleven years old. Valuing both my social and business progression, my father enrolled me in etiquette courses when I was five and spent countless hours instilling me with his strong business ethics and ideals.

My father was an incredible businessman, but even more so, he was an exceptional human being. The ethical and moral values he taught me have always been a guiding light in both my career and personal life—and his vision of a better world continues to inspire me to keep moving the dial forward.

My dad's story is so impactful for me. My dad was a musician from about the age of five years old to twenty, after that he did odd jobs. But when he and my mom got married and were expecting their first child, he was like, "Oh my God, I need to make sure these children are well provided for!" That's when he became motivated to become a CEO. Not just any CEO, but a Fortune 500 CEO.

The amazing thing is, he only had a tenth-grade education. He didn't want to go back to school, but he also didn't want to start at the bottom to work his way up the corporate ladder. He

wanted to find some way of fast tracking it. So, he mapped out all the things that high rankings CEOs and Fortune 500 executives had in common. One stood out. He realized they all had ground transportation in common. Anytime a CEO of Coca-Cola would fly to Vancouver, they had a concierge pick them up and bring them to their appointment.

That was the spark of his business idea. He took out a bank loan and got his first limousine and started a concierge service. When he had the money, he put ads in the white pages. My dad was always a dreamer and a planner. Right from the very beginning he wrote out a business plan, even though he only had $2.25 in his pocket! I remember one time when the bank was looking for his limousine to repossess it. He had been defaulting on his loans. But he ended up raising $1.2 million from one of his wealthy connections in Vancouver. That money launched his limousine company.

BORN TO BE IN BUSINESS

My dad loved to tell the story of giving me my first business lesson when I was three years old. He sat me down and said, "I'm going to teach you everything I'm learning about business because I really need to talk to someone, and I don't have anyone else to talk to."

Back then, there weren't CEO forums. No one really realized the pressure executives were under and how good it is to have a community of people to talk to. My dad started to talk with us, his daughters, to share his business lessons. My sister, was much more rambunctious than I was, grew impatient and ran off. I was more obedient, so I sat there and listened.

If I'm perfectly honest, I'd say that my dad just liked to talk. So, he talked to me—a lot! He told three-year-old me, "By the time you turn twenty-one, you and I are going to write a business plan and go into business together."

By the time I was five, he had seven or eight limousines in his fleet. He was meeting incredible executives and was getting invitations to the boardroom. They were teaching him all about going public and corporate takeovers. He realized early, if his daughter was to be a woman in business, she must have access to any opportunity. To him, that meant etiquette training. My father thought a woman in business should also be a lady. To my luck and slight chagrin, I was put into etiquette classes every single week. I was taught how to walk, talk, and act. The whole book on the head scenario. You name it, we learned it. How to sit properly, how to entertain, set a table, walk like a lady, what cutlery to use, all of it. I had those lessons all the way up until I was sixteen, when I finally had my debutante and I got presented to society.

But back to growing a business. By the time I was eight, he was up to twelve limousines. His business was going great. The more he learned, the more he wanted to share with me. Every time he had someone over to the house to teach him something he'd include me at the "kitchen table meeting." I only realized much later how much I retained and used from those meetings. However, I do remember vividly it was at that very kitchen table that Dad learned about corporate balance sheets, fiduciary responsibilities, and compounding interest rates.

I got excited about becoming a millionaire when I was just eight years old. "If you could save twenty-five dollars a week, by the time you're in your twenties, you'd be a millionaire!" I remember this kitchen table talk the most.

I looked at my dad and asked, "How do I get twenty-five dollars a week?"

He responded, "No, you don't get it, you earn it."

At that moment I declared, "I need to be a millionaire."

WEEKEND WORKSHOP WARRIOR

When I was eleven, my dad decided to sell the limousine company and transition into a different business. He wanted to become an international public speaker. That's when he started attending Jim Rohn workshops. Funny enough, my dad and Tony Robbins were in the same Jim Rohn classes together.

My dad took me along to those weekend workshops. I remember listening intently, feverishly taking notes. I had a pile of them. I just knew I'd go into business when I grew up.

Mr. Rohn would stand on the stage at the end of the weekend say, "Raise your hand if you took five pages of notes. Keep it raised if you took eight pages. How about ten?" People started slowly putting their hands down. By the end, I was the only one with my hand up. He looked at me incredulously and asked, "Could you please come to the front of the room?" I piled up all my note papers, and mind you, I was eleven, so my handwriting was horrible and probably quite big.

I got to the front of the room, and he asked, "How many pages of notes did you take?"

I replied, "Sixteen." I was so proud at that moment.

He asked how old I was. I told him, "I'm eleven."

"You're telling me an eleven-year-old girl took more notes than anybody else in this room? She's going places!" he announced.

I just remember beaming. This first moment I identified a genuine pride of accomplishment. That pride fuelled my first little business.

GOING INTO BUSINESS WITH DAD

Over the next few years, my dad and I attended numerous workshops and, eventually, his dream of becoming an internationally renowned public speaker materialized. He was charging $10,000 for two-day business workshops. He was teaching groups at IBM, Telus, the military, and flying to workshops every other week. His business was exploding. I helped him collate workbooks, sitting in on weekend seminars

of time management, corporate culture, business writing for results—I continued my immersion in business knowledge.

When I turned twenty, my dad declared, "It's time to write that business plan and go into business together."

I still have that company today, Absolute Combustion International (ACI). I was about to be a mom and my dad announced, "We need to develop a technology. A technology that benefits the environment. If it benefits the environment, it's going to benefit the next generation, because we need to make sure they have clean air and water. Make sure they can play in a playground that's not a landfill." Those were very important ideals for him.

After, he came up with a concept for an amazing technology and raised millions of dollars. In early 2015, just before we were about to launch the technology, he passed away. It was devastating. He was my best friend in the world. We traveled together. We worked together. And now he was gone, and I was on my own.

I owe so much to my father's mentorship and the opportunities he provided for me to meet and learn from the greatest business minds in North America—minds like Nido Qubein, George Ross, and J. Abrams. My dad believed strongly in education and mentorship; that's why he was such an amazing mentor himself.

My father's technology only started field tests after he passed. Unfortunately, halfway through our test trial, the recession came along and hit oil and gas. First, I lost my dad, the founder, figurehead, and creator of Absolute Combustion International. Then we lost, our first big potential client. They couldn't put money towards capital expenditures anymore. There were lay-offs across the board. Thankfully, we had amazing shareholders, and I'm grateful for every one of them. They supported us through the struggle to get into the market with a brand-new technology.

MENTORSHIP ENSURES FUTURE SUCCESS

Knowing the power of relationships, I began to network on my own. I started knocking on doors and putting the company and myself out there. I was really pushing myself and meeting lots of people.

I was at a Women in Leadership conference, and I happened to listen to an amazing woman speaker named Suzanne West. I remember she talked about riding her bicycle to get to the conference, how she changed out of her khaki shorts and T-shirt into the cute blue dress she wore to her presentation. She was on stage with this wild lion's mane of a hairstyle. I was captivated. For the first time in my life, I saw a woman on stage who was an engineer and a CEO of an oil and gas company.

She said something simple but so profound it impacts me to this day: "And, not or. You can be a woman in business *and* be a mom. You can be a woman in business *and* be a wife. It doesn't mean you have to choose. You can have both. Look at it as and, not or."

She had such vision I knew immediately that I needed to work with her. I set an intention to get to know her. Eighteen months later, she was my mentor. She also became a shareholder in my company and has been one of the most impactful persons in my life. She also brought me into her company and started her own accelerator, just so she could commercialize my technology.

She gave me my first big contract and she taught me all about people, planet, profit: focus on your people; support the planet; money's always going to come.

Experiencing women in technology and leadership was so powerful. I love the mentorship component because I'd had it my whole life. To be able to work with someone that was such a visionary was an honor.

LOSING, AGAIN

Then, just like my dad, I ended up losing her too. Suzanne passed away in early 2018. It was just a few weeks after I set up our technology for her company. Then the major shareholders from New York decided they didn't like it and they wanted to go in a different direction. They wanted to focus on traditional oil and gas, which meant they didn't like our cleantech on their site. Suzanne had already funded it herself, but her investors wouldn't let it happen. As a precaution, she funded her own accelerator just so she could buy it, and then the company would get the benefit of utilization.

I broke down crying. I'd lost someone else very close and important. Dad passed away in 2015 and Suzanne passed in early 2018. That was a lot for me to handle.

I not only lost my mentor, but the company that took over took out my technology, ripped up my contract, and said, "Too bad, little girl, best of luck to you out there."

BABY BACK BIDS

I was pregnant with my second child, and I wasn't sure what to do. I was crying on the kitchen floor. I had shareholders, responsibilities, and another child coming. My husband wasn't working at the time—the recession was hard on everyone—so it was all on me, supporting my whole family at this point.

Then, out of the blue, I got a phone call from the Alberta government. We had done trade missions with them in the past. They said, "We'd like to sponsor you to go to an aviation conference to promote your technology." I was five months pregnant at the time, so I needed to ask the timeframe. They had the conference set for September. Doing the quick math, I'd have a nine-week-old baby by then. I didn't have a ton of money, so I asked if they could bring someone in from aviation so I could see where my value sat.

They brought the Edmonton International Airport (EIA) to my door, and after they looked at the technology, they said, "We'll talk to you when you get to Japan."

We arrived as a family—husband and kids—and got settled in. It was surreal. I was the only one on the trade mission walking around holding a baby! As a mom and a woman in business, you make do with what you have. If that includes carrying a baby around at a conference, then that is what you do.

SETTING A LIFE TRAJECTORY

It was at that trade mission that the course for my life was set. The mayor, the head pilot, and the EIA took me around the trade show floor, showed me a piece of ground heating equipment for an airplane and asked, "Could you make your technology fit in that?"

I responded, "Absolutely." To be honest, I had no clue if it would. But I was determined to use my mentor Suzanne's words: "And not or."

The mayor gave us the money for our MVP, or minimal viable product. We ended up having 75 percent of the people in the trade mission investing in us.

The airport gave us an amazing lease, made us members of the AATC, and ended up becoming our partners. We co-developed a new product line—got the connections and engagement in the aviation space so we could learn their pain point. They commercialized the technology and endorsed it. They put their logo on it. Their CEO, Tom Ruth, and their VP of Operations, Steve Maybee, and their VP, Myron Keehn, became like family.

I now had three people that I could admire. They all respected and treated me like a person and treated my technology like it was valuable and worthwhile. I made more advancements and developments in aviation that year than all those years of struggle in energy with patronizing men saying, "Oh, little combustion girl, you don't know what you're talking about," doors slamming in my face, and other unsavoury things I don't care to mention.

Instead of slamming doors, EIA opened them. From them, I learned a string of valuable business practices.

Always focus on places you've already hit a home run.

Start in your own province.

Keep your shareholders informed how you are going to sustainably scale so you don't impact quality.

Scale in a way that you never sacrifice customer service or safety.

Steady growth is the best growth.

Always make a positive environmental impact.

Don't work on projects that don't help the environment.

These are axioms I do business by to this day.

RESEARCH AND DEVELOPMENT IN BLOCKCHAIN

Aviation wasn't the only industry I found a home in. Because I'm a total nerd, blockchain caught my attention and I started to research. When it came down to Bitcoin, I couldn't quite comprehend the financial side. I didn't want to get on exchanges. But what I did understand was the mining part. I kept reading white papers and started to build computers. Getting to know cryptography and proof of work, I soon realized scams were everywhere, even falling prey with my own money. So, I would host lunch and learns and teach people how to keep themselves safe in that space, or how to build their own mining equipment so they could save their own money.

I soon became known for supporting a community of learners and that I wasn't asking for anything in return. Before Suzanne passed away, we were already talking about it. She had a great name picked out: The Alberta Blockchain Consortium. She called it her ABC and she wanted to figure out how to use it to support the energy sector. How do we make better efficiencies? How could this support the environment?

A gentleman named James Graham, President and CEO, GuildOne Inc. asked me to help him create something out of ABC, to ensure Suzanne's legacy was remembered. I was already keeping ACI going for my dad, and now I had the opportunity with ABC to build this incredible woman's legacy. I took on ABC and incorporated it as a not for profit. I was so passionate about it that I self-funded it with a quarter million dollars. It's now officially called the Canadian Blockchain Consortium and it is the largest industry organization in Canada on blockchain.

ABC, now CBC, has been my volunteer project, off the side of my desk. If there was a way I could honor Suzanne, I would do it. I am proud, because I've been able to merge my worlds, which is beautiful. It combines my passions for tech, supporting women in tech, and advocating for this awesome blockchain ecosystem. It truly has been an incredible experience.

A FEMALE ELON MUSK

I have had so many opportunities in my life I love to help others have those same opportunities. Through the Edmonton airport, I started to work with a group called Elevate Aviation. Elevate Aviation teaches girls in high school all about combustion and how that supports aviation. I remember having a young girl look at me with big wondrous eyes, blurting, "You're like a female Elon Musk." It was such a cool moment. Plus, I love it because it got their brains thinking and wondering...what could I do in this space?

I became the vice chair of Elevate Aviation's board because of their CEO, Kendra Kincade. I have been so very blessed meeting great mentors and Kendra is like another Suzanne. She's inspirational, humble, and authentic. She has accomplished a great deal, and I am grateful to work on the board alongside her.

TAPPING INTO YOUR PAST TO INVENT YOUR FUTURE

Absolute Combustion International spent its first three years trying to come up with a business that brought environmental technology to the world so humans could clean up their mess. We tried partnering with inventors, admitting we weren't engineers or inventors of technology, but stressing we understood business, fundraising, and marketing. And we got a few opportunities to partner with some amazing visionaries. It was a unique and eye-opening experience. Inventors are fascinating, brilliant, and often wildly creative people.

But many inventors remind me of Smeagol from *The Lord of the Rings*. Their technology was The Precious, and they were obsessed with it. Unfortunately, they never seemed ready to launch a product, nor did they ever seem to want to leave the safe haven of the lab.

Talking about building and inventing, I can't help but think of my dad and his incredible experience with the invention process. My family has indigenous peoples on both my mother's and father's side. My dad had a passion for healing our communities and the planet, but he didn't know how or in what way.

We had elders living close by and my dad asked one of them for guidance. Sequoia offered to help and took him out into the woods and did a sweat-lodge ceremony with him. This is a spiritual journey and ritual for healing and prayer practiced by many indigenous peoples. The ritual is often used to find answers and trigger insights and visions.

Two days later, my dad woke me up in the middle of the night and told me he had a profound dream. He described it like *Star Trek*'s holographic projector. This beam of light came down like a nozzle, an inner working of something. He said he couldn't wake up until he memorized everything. The striation, the depth, the look, everything about it. He drew it on a napkin. My dad wasn't a very good illustrator, so we were very confused as to what we were looking at.

We took it to a good friend who was an expert at technology. He looked at the napkin of my dad's dream. Like my dad, this friend was also quite spiritual, and he appreciated the emphasis my dad was putting on intuition. He asked, "Where is the nozzle going? Is it going to a burner?"

My dad said to him, "Let's build a burner."

We went to a community that supports healing, self-improvement, and the environment and raised three million dollars. We called it *love money* because it's from people who love the idea of healing our communities. The first contribution was a hundred-thousand-dollar cheque from a woman that declared, "Go live your dream and let's just see what it does." She's given us a million dollars to date.

THE BURNER LOVE BUILT

We built a "burner thing" that looked like a tin can with holes in it. We built it in our garage, with our passions, dreams, and visions to help people and planet. We started in 2009, worked through a recession, then hit another one in 2014 before finally launching our aviation project in 2020.

The Absolute Extreme Burner™ is a game-changing evolution of standard combustion burners with the power to transform industrial heating and power generation. Cool enough to touch and with a near-flameless combustion process, the technology provides combustion with lower emissions and reduced fuel consumption.

After all the struggle and time, we had the win-win we wanted. It's been a wild ride, but I wouldn't have missed it for the world.

PIVOTING DURING COVID-19

Of course, there was another big moment that happened in 2020.

I've had many crying-on-the-floor moments in my entrepreneurial journey. If it wasn't for my mentorships, personal development, and amazing coaches, I don't know if I would have come out of all my challenges as strong as I am.

Every time I hit a new roadblock I thought, all right, it's an obstacle, but it's also an opportunity. We can do this. How do we shift our thinking? How do we move through this?

When COVID-19 hit, it was a challenge. Thank goodness for all the amazing people supporting us. We were able to pivot and take the product we made for aviation, redesign a new product line with a complete company rebrand for the construction industry, and built out a rental fleet.

BUSINESS JOY

The pivoting triumphs aside, what I enjoy most about business is the education. I like to think every dollar I've raised has gone towards my education. At this point, I have a nine-million-dollar PhD.

I've learned a lot about myself, and I've had many humbling experiences along the way. I've learned how to engage with people, interact with people, energize people, and energize myself. I'm very much like my dad. He wanted to absorb information and education all the time. As for me, I was never a traditional learner. I was more hands-on, so I didn't make it through the academic route. I made it through the *education by life* route.

Right now, my hobbies are economics and learning about the history of cigars. I can tell you a lot of interesting things about cigars!

A JOURNEY OF "NO" TO GET TO "YES"

I would say the key ability for an entrepreneur is how well you handle rejection. If you're the type that hears "No," cries, and quits, then this life is not for you. You know you're a true entrepreneur when you hear "No" and you tell yourself "I don't care if I hear a thousand."

Entrepreneurs have the confidence to know that at some point they're going to hear a "Yes." It doesn't matter if you're a man or a woman, it's the confidence to keep going that counts. It's the belief in what you're doing. It doesn't matter how many people say "No," or don't agree with your vision or believe it. You believe it enough yourself that you're going to move it forward. I believe the confidence that handles rejection is the biggest critical piece to success.

As an entrepreneur, you will hear more answers that sound like No than sound like Yes. But, instead of quitting, the entrepreneur takes each No and starts asking questions.

What do I need to do to create that Yes?

Every time someone says No, it's a lesson. What am I going to learn from this?

Why did they say No?

How do I have to change the business or the offering?

Do I have to make something better, so the next time I get a No, it's a lesser No?

The people who can take a journey of No's to get to Yes know how to shift and modify obstacles into opportunities. They stick with it, whether the journey is two years or fifteen.

ADVICE FOR WOMEN IN BUSINESS

My absolute favourite quote in the whole wide world is one by Arlene Dickinson: "May all women have the confidence of a middle-aged white man."

Dickinson's reasoning came from women's ingrained lack of confidence. To paraphrase a famous example, if women see a job posting that lists ten qualifications, and they don't hit all ten check marks, they think they can't do the job. That they're not good enough. So, they don't even apply. A man sees that job posting, and he hits four or five of those qualifications, he's like, all right, cool, I'll give it a shot.

There's a certain confidence men have. They're willing to put themselves out there. They're willing to try more. They're willing to ask for a raise. Their confidence is strong.

Women tend to be more timid. We are usually brought up that way.

This can have an advantage. Women are great to lend money to because they're so risk adverse. They won't take a penny unless they know they're going to pay 100 percent of it back. But they're also unwilling to take good risks. They need to build up confidence. It's those women who take the risk that get the reward. You want to be able to gain access to those incredible rewards.

How do we build up that courage? In my opinion, it's a self-work piece. It's learning how to shift your thinking to create self-confidence.

Repeat these mantras: I am competent. I am capable. I am deserving. I can do this. I might not have 100 percent of these skillsets, but I'm willing to learn. I'll put myself out there.

I knew zero about combustion when I started, but I was willing to learn. I knew less than zero about Bitcoin and blockchain, but I was willing to learn. I knew nothing about sitting on a board, but I was willing to learn. I knew nothing about business, but I was willing to learn. I didn't know anything about public speaking, but I was willing to learn.

My passions made me want to learn. I might not understand it right now and you might ask me a question I can't answer, but I'll figure it out for you because I'm not going to B.S. somebody. What you put out there is your willingness to learn and try.

BUILDING PRIDE IN MYSELF

Years ago, when I was at that Women in Leadership conference and first heard Suzanne West speak, my assistant encouraged me to get out and do some networking. I was very nervous. I thought, what do I have to offer? I don't know anybody. Who's going to want to talk to me? Our company is so small. I was very intimidated. Even my clothing choice was cause for anxiety. I went out and got a pantsuit. Then I wondered, if I wear a pantsuit, am I going to look like a ballbuster? I didn't even know how to approach someone to say hi.

Then Suzanne shows up riding a bike and wearing khaki shorts. I had to psyche myself up to ask her a question. "How can a woman in business still be feminine? If you're too feminine, men will think you're just a pretty face. If you're too much of a man, they'll call you a ballbuster."

She shrugged, "It doesn't matter what you wear. It doesn't matter how you look. What matters is, do you know your stuff? That's it. You can be a woman and be anything you want in business, as long as you know your stuff."

I was so in awe of her. I kept telling myself, "I'm going to work with her. I must work with her." I had worked with my therapist to set this intention. I was so nervous when I finally got that first meeting with her. When I partnered with Suzanne West, I was grateful and proud. I had set that intention, worked hard, and believed in myself.

That newfound confidence would blossom into my superpower: my ability to inspire others with my vision and ideas to get buy-in.

THE ORIGINAL WOMAN WHO KNEW HER STUFF

If I had a historical mentor, it would be U.S. Supreme Court Justice Ruth Bader Ginsburg. She was such a badass. Back then, making it work as a woman required tenacity. Absolute and utter tenacity. I've read her life's work. I've seen the movies on her. And I'm in awe. Her husband had cancer. She was going through Harvard. She was not respected as a female, or as a lawyer. She had children and she made it work. She killed it.

What she was able to do for women to set a precedent in such a time is part of the reason I'm able to do what I do today. She was absolutely glorious. I want to thank her so much. When you look back in history it's women like her who helped me break those glass ceilings. And glass ceilings break for everyone, not just women. One of her cases argued that an unmarried man, as a caregiver, could have access to tax rebates he needed to support himself and his infirm mother.

After Ginsburg, I would absolutely love to talk to whoever the heck Satoshi Nakamoto was, the pseudonym person or persons who developed Bitcoin and authored the white paper. Simply because of the brilliance of understanding cryptography, proof of work, Austrian economics, and geopolitical politics. I bow and tip my hat to you, Satoshi, who created the soundest money the world has ever seen and one of my deepest passions.

THE SECRET TO BALANCING WORK AND LIFE AS A MOTHER, A WIFE, AND AN ENTREPRENEUR

I've been divorced twice. Honestly, I have to say the secret to balancing work and life is who you choose for a partner.

That's the power of teamwork. Of partnership.

It's rare to find a true life partner. In my experience, husbands are either intimidated by you or they try to push you down. I'm not saying that everyone does this, but it's hard in a patriarchal society to find a mate that actively supports the balance you want to keep.

KOLEYA'S TOP TRAVEL DESTINATIONS

When I do get away, I have a short list of places I love to go. Number one, Japan. I love Japan. I've been there twice. They are the kindest people I have ever met, and I always felt safe. In a city of thirty-six million people, I could go for a walk in the evening and not have a single concern. Plus, it's a beautiful and stunning country.

My next favourite city in the world is New Orleans. I'm considered Creole because I'm black, French, and native. The food is amazing there. I would be 300 pounds if I lived in New Orleans because of the food. But I love the history and somehow, I feel like I'm home. I don't know why, but just that feeling of being home. That's one of those places for me.

I would also love to visit the Tuscany area in Italy. I've never been there but I am absolutely dying to go. I watched the movie *Under the Tuscan Sun* as a young girl and fell in love with the area and I love a good red wine.

TREATING MYSELF

Aside from travel, my other big treat to myself is cigars. Cigars are one of my hobbies, after all. I do love cigars.

When I am in Edmonton, I go to Q Cigar. I'm a VIP member. I have been going there for years. Their steak and cigars are awesome. Many people comment, "I don't think I've met anyone else in Q's lounge that knows as much about cigars as you do." I even have my own cigar box with my name on it.

KOLEYA'S ENTREPRENEURIAL BUCKET LIST

I have two things on my business bucket list I hope to accomplish over the next three to five years. First, a hundred of my newest units being used in the market within five years. That would be an audacious goal and would make us a hundred-million-dollar company. That, and for my Canadian Blockchain Consortium to put Canada on the map for blockchain innovation. I want Canada to be recognized as one of the world's top ten leaders in blockchain.

PARTING WORDS OF WISDOM

As for my final words, I say this: belief creates the world. Believe you can achieve whatever business success you want, and you'll create it.

Koleya Karringten, a Canadian entrepreneur in the field of blockchain technology, has garnered recognition for her diverse roles as an ecosystem leader, published author, and public speaker.

Within Alberta's burgeoning blockchain community, Karringten stands out as a prominent figure, advocating for the vast economic and social possibilities tied to digital transformation. In her capacity as the Executive Director of the Canadian Blockchain Consortium she actively promotes the potential of blockchain technology.

10

Perseverance Hits the Nail on the Head
Henri Rodier and Coventry Homes

B ACK IN THE SUMMER OF 2021, A FRIEND AND respected business leader, Amir Shami, President & CEO of Rotaflow Fire & Utility, told me that he planned on making an introduction as one of his TEC (The Executive Committee) Canada forum members was potentially interested in utilizing the services that we offer at X5 Management.

The introduction was made, and Henri Rodier, President and CEO of Coventry Homes, and I scheduled a luncheon meeting to discuss how we could potentially support their business.

Henri and I are both comfortable in a conversation and our first meeting was no different, as we comfortably connected and learned that we had a commonality of being Saskatchewan born farm boys.

Within weeks, I had started to work with Henri and his team.

Over 47 years ago, Henri and his wife Yvette started a home building company which evolved into the company they know today, Coventry Homes, which is part of the Coventry Group of Companies. Little did they know at that time what lay ahead of them—the challenges, setbacks and victories. After 47+ years of progress in an exciting industry, what lays ahead of them in the future? Henri is proud of the team that they have put together and he looks forward to taking on the challenges, and in Henri's words, "There is so much more we can accomplish and will accomplish."

In 1976, Henri, Yvette and former business partners founded HRS Construction, which became Champagne Homes and eventually Coventry Homes. As an Edmonton based, family owned and operated business, they offer a variety of customizable floorplans to suit home buyers needs and lifestyles. As a company they are devoted to building confidence and creating peace of mind.

Over the company's 47-year history, Coventry Homes has achieved several notable milestones.

- In 1990 the company was awarded the prestigious title of "CHBA Edmonton, Builder of the Year."

- The Coventry Homes Adoption Gallery was built in the Edmonton Humane Society in recognition of the partnership and contributions in 2005.
- Received the JD Power "Builder of Excellence" award in 2013.
- Became the Preferred Builder of the Edmonton Oilers® in 2015; recently became the Official Builder of the Edmonton Oilers®
- Awarded the Ernst and Young Entrepreneur of the Year Award in 2016
- In 2018, Coventry Homes built and donated a home to Habitat for Humanity
- Awarded the "Leadership Award" at the 2020 CHBA, Edmonton Awards of Excellence
- Awarded 2022 Builder of the Year

It was a pleasure to sit down with Henri and learn about his leadership and entrepreneurial journey, and I look forward to having all readers better understand Henri's journey as a leader and entrepreneur.

FAMILY ROOTS

I'm from a town of 300 in Saskatchewan called Arborfield. I'm the oldest of 10 siblings and I grew up on the family farm that was passed down from my grandfather to my father. I went to school in Zenon Park at a convent for three years because they didn't have school buses. Even though we lived in Arborfield, I went to Zenon Park, a French town, because I was of French descent and most of my relatives were there.

When I was 20 years old, I lost my father and youngest brother in a plane crash that my father was piloting. It was a devastating time for my mother and our family. As the oldest son, I had to grow up fast; this was one of my early pivotal moments in my life that really impacted who I was and who I needed to become.

EARLY ASPIRATIONS

Growing up in a small town, you have plenty of time to figure out what you want to do. And, for some reason, I always wanted to be an archaeologist. But, until I could do that, I started playing the bass guitar, and my brother played rhythm guitar. We got a couple of other guys from town together and played at school dances. In 1970, we moved to Saskatoon, where I went for one year of university. We played all around Saskatoon and decided to go on the road, which meant playing nightclubs, bars, lounges. We ended up doing the circuit across Canada. We played from 1971 until 1976 on the circuit and ended up doing over 2,500 different gigs. Those five years were what we called our "professional years" because that's how we made our living. We continued playing in Edmonton and the area until 1986, a total of 16 years from our start in 1970.

During our professional years, our band, "Gates of Dawn", recorded an album and a single that was only locally released. It wasn't anything national, but today, with YouTube, it is there for anyone to listen to. We did play for a long time, and that's what brought us to Edmonton because we were in the music business. When we were here playing at the Kingsway Garden Inn, there was talk about a mall com-

ing in right beside the King-sway Garden Inn. We loved playing music, but our end game had always been to start up a business, prefera-bly in the music industry.

At that time, we'd already invested in some houses, an alfalfa plant up in Falher, Alberta. Our next big plans

Henri is on the far left.

were to settle down where we could start the business, which ended up being Edmonton because of the Kingsway Garden Mall opening.

MY FIRST BUSINESS

Our first business was a retail store called Mr. Entertainment in Kingsway Garden Mall and we sold musical instruments, musi-cal sheets, and it was the mid '70s. At that time there weren't big players in the business yet, so it looked like we were going to revolutionize the music world by bringing in something from Japan called a CD. Our plan was to lock up the contract for the distribution of CDs in Canada.

Well, of course we all know now that it doesn't work that way. We did end up selling some CDs, but we didn't have the distribution for Canada. The good thing was that got us settled into Edmonton.

Here we were with this one store owned by four guys in the band. Two guys ran the store, and there were two guys that were left looking for a day job—Lou and myself. We all ended up playing every night at the Kingsway Garden Inn for two years after we got finished with our day jobs.

Lou and I started looking around the area for more opportunities, and thought construction looked like a really good thing to get into. In 1976, construction was going crazy in Edmonton. We started as apprentice carpenters with Murray Tetlock, an uncle of Dan, our lead guitar player. We started framing houses and still playing at night. Over a period of time, we got to know people that were in the industry; about two months in, we were approached to start our own framing company, and hire ourselves out as a framing crew. So that's what we did.

THE STARTUP PROCESS

With just our pouches, hammers, and a modest sum of money, we each contributed $50 to a collective fund to purchase equipment and start a framing crew. We subcontracted ourselves to larger framing operations, taking on specialized tasks such as building stairwells and landings.

For Lou and me, music was our first passion. Yet, we were quickly acquiring construction skills, thanks to Dieter, a master carpenter who joined us and shared his extensive knowledge.

By February 1976, we had laid down our roots in Edmonton and were honing our carpentry skills. We founded HRS Construction in June of the same year with the three of us at the helm. Upon our arrival in February, along with the other band members, we purchased a fourplex in St. Albert, Alberta—a duplex with two basement suites that became our shared home. All four of us were committed to making it work; we juggled playing music at night with carpentry or running Mr. Entertainment by day. The year 1976 was a whirlwind of activity.

Our break came unexpectedly when, after only three days working on a 36-suite apartment building, the owner dismissed the lead framer due to poor performance and significant delays. Learning that we had a master carpenter among us, he entrusted us with the leadership of the framing crew to complete the project. It was late July 1976, and that moment marked the beginning of our journey in the construction business.

BUSINESS BEGINNINGS

We completed several apartment and townhome projects before heading to Glendon, Alberta, where we spent a month managing the construction of a UFA (United Farmers of Alberta) building. Upon our return to Edmonton, we expanded our framing crew to 12 to 14 workers. Over two years, we undertook projects primarily for companies like Nu West and Cairns, focusing on four-level apartments. However, our ultimate goal was to transition from framing to home building.

In 1978, the land in Edmonton was monopolized by major builders, so we purchased a lot in Legal, Alberta, and constructed our first bi-level house of 1,000 square feet on speculation. It sold quickly due to the favourable market. Our second build was more personal; we moved from St. Albert to an acreage and built a four-level split house with a four-car garage. Lou occupied the lower levels, and my family, which had grown to five, took the upper levels.

After about two years, we parted ways with our third partner, Dieter, who couldn't bear the cold and suffered from back problems making physical labour challenging for him. Lou and I had learned enough to proceed on our own, so we brought on a lead framer to further our education. Within a year, we were leading the projects, laying out plans and overseeing the work. During this period, we also constructed a few more houses in an area known as Hess Estates.

FROM FRAMERS TO BUILDERS

Just as we started building houses, the early 1980s brought a market crash, which actually presented an opportunity for us as a small builder. Without the hefty costs that drove many large builders to bankruptcy, we were well-positioned to fill the void in Edmonton's construction scene. A chance encounter with Shell Oil provided a breakthrough; they had reclaimed about 100 lots from bankrupt builders in Londonderry Meadows, north Edmonton.

I traveled to Toronto with Taras Chmil, a realtor friend, to negotiate with Shell Oil. We struck a deal to establish a show home in Londonderry with exclusive rights to the lots, deferring payment until we handed homes over to buyers, allowing us to build on demand.

In 1982, we collaborated with another builder to erect our first show home. At that time, government incentives were promoting apartment construction. We capitalized on this, completing a 24-suite apartment building in Morinville by 1983. Meanwhile, our house sales were climbing, averaging eight to ten a year, alongside maintaining a full framing crew.

During the frenetic period of the mid-70s and early 80s in Edmonton, adept negotiation was crucial. The initial housing boom attracted a rush of builders, but the subsequent market slump saw them eager to exit, leaving room for us to negotiate further deals. We secured 36 lots with Cadillac Fairview in the West Lynburn subdivision. By 1984, the market had started to recover, with houses priced around $100,000 and lots at $17,000. Interest rates, having peaked at 18%, began to stabilize at about 12.75%, reinvigorating the market and consumer interest.

DIFFICULT LESSONS

By 1989 and '90, our diligent efforts had paid off, and we became Edmonton's second-largest builder, trailing only behind Reid

Built Homes. In 1990, we were honored with the Edmonton Home Builders Builder of the Year award, an accolade that took us by surprise. We had progressed from constructing four or five homes in the mid-80s to completing over 250 home sales annually by 1990. However, our rapid growth led to overextension and cash flow issues as we couldn't build and sell homes quickly enough.

The 'handshake' partnership with Lou came to an end in 1994 following his marriage, leading to the division of our company. That same year, as I took the helm as President of the Home Builders, I also navigated the complex process of splitting, selling, or dissolving the 17 companies we had formed together. Without a Unanimous Shareholder Agreement (USA), the separation was challenging and costly, with legal fees reaching half a million dollars—a substantial amount at the time.

After the dust settled, we found ourselves back at square one, with 15 years of experience but little financial equity. Lou took a smaller portion of the business, moved to St. Albert, and established Soucy Homes. Meanwhile, I took over the larger share of the company. It was then that I faced the reality that I could not retain the name Champagne Homes, a brand we had built since 1982 known for its stellar reputation. The valuation of the name was contentious—it was deemed worthless if Lou assumed it, yet valued at one and a half million dollars in my hands. Opting against an unreasonable payout, I decided to rebrand. Thus, Coventry Homes was born, marking a fresh start in 1994.

STARTING OVER

In the aftermath of our financial struggles, I refinanced my house, as our cash flow had dwindled to practically nothing, leaving me with a net worth deep in the red. The legal battles had drained our resources in just one year. We scaled back considerably, securing a modest office on 107th Avenue and 181st Street and reducing operations significantly. From the myriad of divisions in the latter days of Champagne Homes, I downsized to four, with the deliberate intention to maintain a manageable scope. Despite being battered and weary, I decided to build no more than 45 to 50 homes annually, working alone without partners for safety and simplicity.

This conservative approach was manageable and allowed for a gradual increase in production—from 40 homes in our first year to a steady rise to 75. During the split, we had to negotiate with our subcontractors, setting up a three-year plan to settle debts with monthly installments. Both Lou and I honored our separate obligations, and within two and a half years, I had cleared all dues. The tradespeople showed remarkable loyalty, a testament to our prior relationship, enabling us to avoid any bankruptcies and simply work through the debt.

By 1997, the entrepreneurial fire was rekindled within me, and I began to cautiously expand operations. Those initial three to four years were grueling, but they set a strong foundation for growth.

Reflecting on the division of Champagne Homes in 1994, we faced the daunting task of disentangling 17 different business ventures without a Unanimous Shareholder Agreement (USA) to guide us. The lack of a USA loomed over us, with the constant threat of bankruptcy used as leverage during negotiations. Despite these challenges and the ongoing threats, we managed to settle the affairs of most companies, with a few being acquired by other partners. It was a complex and arduous process, but ultimately, we succeeded in navigating through it.

GETTING HONEST WITH MYSELF

Champagne Homes was basically feeding most of these companies, and we weren't making money from them. We just had companies doing different things in real estate, brokerage inventions and different things like that. My thought was to keep it to one company, and make sure that company was strong. That's where I put all my effort.

KEEPING THE BUSINESS IN THE FAMILY

At that point, Coventry Homes started to grow, and by 2000, we were back in the game. We were one of the top 20 builders again. We were in seven or eight subdivisions. By the time 2006 rolled around, we were doing over 200–250 houses. At that time, my children started to become interested in working for the company. I have a daughter and two sons. My daughter moved to Toronto for her job and has done super over there, but my two sons, one of them, my youngest son, Mark, started with the company in

April 2003. He had been working for a friend of mine for a few years in the hot tar roofing business. After having a number of conversations with him, I told him it was up to him which direction he wanted to go. Mark started working in the Customer Care department and worked his way up to being the President today. He's been with the company for 20 years and has basically worked his way up right from the bottom. My other son, Raymond, when he was 18, started framing for some framing crews that were working for us, learning the trade of being a framer, kind of like how his dad started. Within about two years, he had his own framing crew and framed for us for many years. The company was called Titan Framing. Framing is a very hard job, and in 2004, about four years after he'd started his own crew, I suggested he and his mother start a housing company, and that we would work with them. That's where Impact Homes comes from.

COMBINING COMPANIES

Raymond and Yvette had been growing Impact Homes, and by 2007, when we moved into our new building, we had Impact

Homes join us there. Over the years, we've amalgamated the two companies so that we're a group of companies with a few other companies involved. We didn't go crazy with 17 companies this time, but we have companies that support the main companies. It worked out well.

BRINGING IN CAPABLE PEOPLE

I have changed a lot since 1994 when we restarted with Coventry Homes. At that time, I wanted to do everything myself. In 2005, I started looking at minority shareholders, selling some of the company off, and having partners. I love having partners. I love working with people, collaborating, and getting ahead. It's a lot easier when you've got partners to help you with your vision versus going it alone.

In 2005, we started selling little pieces of the company to some of the key executives. It's no longer just a Rodier family business; it's a family business, but there are more families in it.

That's the way that I look at it: it's a family business for all the families that are involved in the ownership.

I learned a very expensive lesson with my partner and the past split up. In 2005, I put together a very good USA (Unanimous Shareholders Agreement). Now if one of my partners does pass away, or decides to move on, it's simple to figure out exactly how to buy back those shares. I get to buy back any shares when people leave the company and then I get to redistribute them to people I think that would be a good team member.

In 2007, we had trouble finding proper trades. It was a tough time because we had too many sales and not enough people to build homes, but it put us over the top as far as financially and put us in a very good spot to progress in the marketplace. We moved up into the top 10 builders in town and have been there and above ever since.

COMMUNITY AND ACCOLADES

We collaborated with the Edmonton Humane Society and became their major sponsor in 2005 to build their building on 137th Avenue. We're the major sponsor there and we're the sponsor for the adoption centre. We've done 13 galas for them since that date. We had committed $500,000 back in 2005. Once we reached that goal, we just continued. We're currently sitting at $1.8 million that we've raised for the Edmonton Humane Society.

Then in 2015, we became the Preferred Builder of the Edmonton Oilers. That changed how people looked at us; associating the Oilers brand with our brand took us to the top level in our industry.

In 2013, we ended up getting a J.D. Power Builder of Excellence.

In 2021, we hit 5,000 homes for Coventry and 250 homes for

Impact. For the group of companies, we're probably around that 5,500 homes, 5,600 homes right now.

THE ENTREPRENEURIAL SPIRIT

I probably always had an entrepreneurial spirit, but when I was playing in the band, I was the youngest, and I basically followed along. When we moved into Edmonton and two members went to Mr. Entertainment, we started in construction. When they built the second store, they wanted us to join them and be under them as apprentices, but we wouldn't be involved as owners in the second store for some reason. We'd already been in our construction business for a few years so, we declined and sold out our shares of Mr. Entertainment. We were in charge of our own destiny now.

I think just struggling to make things work *made* me become a leader. I needed to set up the company and start bringing in revenue. It just seemed natural to me. I never thought about "being an entrepreneur" at the time, or that I was doing anything other than just making sure I could feed my family.

GROWTH STRUGGLES

One of the problems in our business was growth, which had started before my 1994 split with my partner. We were always discussing whether we should grow or stay small. Growing was out of his comfort zone but was part of my DNA.

That struggle due to growth came to a head in 1994 and allowed me to chase my dreams.

One, I now had full authority to do what I wanted with the new company as I was the sole owner. And two, I could bring in my family as they grew older, because now they were teenagers and that would've been difficult with a partner the way it was.

No longer having a partner allowed me to be able to design the company around the family, control the growth, set up the family trust and get my sons involved. They came in willingly. I did not push them into it. I think they're very embedded in the progress of the company.

ADVICE FOR ASPIRING ENTREPRENEURS

Persistence and perseverance are what's going to get you to where you want to go. You must look at the ups and the downs and keep them level if you can. You're going to have some tough times. You're going to have some good times. Don't go crazy on your good times and don't get too down on your bad times. You've got to know that your business will go up and down. There will be things that you'll wonder why they happened, and when you look back, you'll see that a lot of times, it happened for the right reason.

You have to be solid in where you are going. You must also work with people, listen to people, take advice, all those things that make a company strong.

When you're getting started, you're going to find out that sometimes it looks hopeless. It looks like you're not going anywhere, but what I always tell everybody is, "All you have to do is look back three years, look back five years. Are you ahead of where you were then? Sometimes the progress looks slow, but when you look back, you will see you've come a long way in those five years. You must also always be looking forward. Focusing on what you're trying to accomplish and not get discouraged by setbacks. Setbacks are all part of the learning experience."

Another important piece of advice is to make sure you make good use of any downturns. A downturn is the best time for your business to move forward, and you'll always see tons of opportunities in a downturn, whereas there are fewer opportunities in an upturn.

We made huge steps in the downturns of 2008 and 2015. Those downturns are what catapulted us from being in the top 20 to the top 10 and from the top 10 to the top 5, because we looked at the opportunities that other people were passing up.

MY GREATEST STRENGTH

I'm collaborative. I like to work with everyone and get everybody's opinion and listen to what they have to say. I also try to stay the path and move forward; I definitely have perseverance, but I love the team, and teamwork. When you start out, you often start out on your own—but as you grow, you must start looking at how a strong team can make you and the company that much stronger.

THE IMPORTANCE OF OUTSIDE PERSPECTIVE

In 2005, I joined TEC (The Executive Committee) as a forum member, and it has been a turning point in my business life. It has taught me so many things because I'm with my peers and fellow entrepreneurs. We discuss things openly and it all stays inside the room. One of the things is when you're an entrepreneur, sometimes it can get kind of lonely because there's only a limited amount of people, if any, that you can talk about your problems to, without them either getting scared or wondering where you're coming from.

When you go into that TEC room, you can trust everyone in there. There are so many educational factors that come with it; there's so many things that we do in our company today that came from TEC, from speakers about how to run your company to advice and perspective on how to look at things. TEC has been a huge part of my personal growth.

I can't overstate TEC, actually. I just can't. It changed the way I think about a lot of things and opened up my mind to all kind of new ways of dealing with personalities, issues, and challenges.

FOCUS AND SUCCESSION PLANNING

I think a lot of leaders misjudge how long it will take for them to figure out succession. It takes a long time, and it is a moving target, but you need to start early so that you can start to figure it out in your mind where you think it should go. Yes, it might be different by the time you get there, but at least you've been on the road and on the route of getting there. Also, I think using the knowledge of the people around you. Get opinions, listen to them, get experienced people to help you out on certain things that you're not experienced at. There's lots of good people that can help you get to where you want to be. You're not the only person who knows something.

FIVE-YEAR BUCKET LIST

The bucket list for me is instituting more inclusive ownership into our group of companies.

The other bucket list thing I would want for the company is to see some of our legacy projects completed and see how they look. I guess personally, I'd love to be able to see where the third generation starts to get worked into the group of companies. When I say that, I'm not necessarily just saying my grandchildren, but possibly also children of some of the other owners. It's already happening with some of our staff; some of our people have children or spouses who work for us.

DEFINITION OF SUCCESS

I define success as feeling good about what you've done and accomplished. I don't have a monetary figure on it; it's more about personal satisfaction about what you've done and accomplished, and also what you've done for your community.

Also, success is what you leave behind. What do you leave behind more than your family? To me, that's a measurement of success—trying to have children and grandchildren that grow up to be good people.

From humble beginnings, Coventry Homes has grown to be recognized as a leading home builder in the Edmonton area. We've taken great pride in growing our team with exceptional people who have become part of the Coventry Family and working with thousands of families to make their dream homes a reality.

That's the way I see success.

HARD WORK EQUALS SUCCESS

Don't sell yourself short. We live in a country where basically just about anything can be accomplished. Your destiny is guided by your hand for the most part, not like in some other parts of the world where you are where you are, and you're never going to get out of that. You should make sure that you appreciate that. That's number one.

Number two, I would say always move forward. Sometimes you don't know where you're going but move forward to one thing and then from there, move forward to another thing and don't get depressed that it can take too long. Just continue to push forward and then you can look back and see how you've made out.

Too many people want to have success too fast.

Success comes with good, hard work. It comes with perseverance. It comes with planning. It comes with thinking things through, and it comes with confidence in yourself.

Don't sell yourself short. If you want to be an entrepreneur, just start the process and it'll happen, but if you don't have that courage, because it does take some courage to do that, then make sure you get a good job and get some good education. You might find out later that you do want to be an entrepreneur but start someplace.

LEADERS I ADMIRE

I had a ton of respect for the late Bill Bagshaw, who was my TEC Chair for 15 years. Bill passed away in July 2023 at 91 years of age and worked right up to his passing. I look back at him and think, "That is a real good life." That's someone who doesn't just check out at some point. I guess I'm not trying to suggest that you can't stop—people do retire! What I am saying is that age doesn't have to impede your passion and enthusiasm on continuing to be productive and engaged in life.

Awhile back, I read a book by Eddie Jaku, a holocaust survivor from Auschwitz. He died in the fall of 2021 at the age of 101. In his book, *The Happiest Man on Earth: The Beautiful Life of an Auschwitz Survivor*, he goes all through his life and his challenges, and the light that he still had after going through hell for so many years.

I think, "Holy cow!" It's so impressive to be able to go through all that and still end up having a life that he is doing so many things and ending up with such a wonderful family.

Perhaps I connected with the book as I too believe in perseverance, resilience and seeing the positive side of life and business. It's not always easy, but I get up each morning with that goal in mind.

FINAL WORDS OF WISDOM

When we started the company back in 1976, part of that company was my wife, Yvette. She started with me doing everything. She was the secretary, she was the bookkeeper, she was everything, and I was out in the field; she was part of this whole journey for over 40 years. I think a lot of people would say, "Wow, you worked with your wife for 40 years. How the hell did you do that?"

Well, you know what? It was just natural for us. It worked out just fantastic. She is a great person and partner. She did retire a few years ago, but she was a huge part of the success of the company. That was the start of the family business, I guess, right there. It was always about family.

Henri Rodier is the CEO of Coventry Homes, which he founded in 1976 along with his wife Yvette. Henri and the company have contributed to the community and also enjoyed success and awards over the years, including: CHBA Edmonton, Builder of the Year 1990; Henri was the President of the Canadian Home Builders Association—Edmonton Region in 1994; The Coventry Homes Adoption Gallery was built in the Edmonton Humane Society in recognition of the partnership and contributions in 2005; JD Power "Builder of Excellence" award in 2013; became the Preferred Builder of the Edmonton Oilers in 2015, and in 2023, Coventry Homes became the Official Builder of the Edmonton Oilers®; Ernst and Young Entrepreneur of the Year Award in 2016; in 2018, Coventry Homes built and donated a home to Habitat for Humanity; Leadership Award 2020 CHBA, Edmonton Awards of Excellence; and 2022 Builder of the Year, in the large volume category.

11

Token Leaders

Keenan Pascal and
Token Naturals

I T'S HARD TO BELIEVE THAT I FIRST MET KEENAN WAY back in late 2009 through a former business connection of mine. Over the years we would run into each other and have some meaningful dialogue about life and business. In recent years we both became affiliated with a group of business leaders in Edmonton and there, we can get caught up on a somewhat more regular basis. Every time we interact, he brings such a pleasant, calm, and humble approach to every networking event or conversation. As we will learn in this chapter, Keenan applies that approach to his business as well.

For the record, Keenan is our youngest leader in my book, but don't let his age be a factor, as the rich wisdom that he has brought to Lunch with Leaders is evident. I would also add that he has a late addition to the book, due some complications with another chapter and when I reached out to Keenan, he didn't hesitate for a moment and graciously offered his time to meet with me, within 24 hours after returning from a Mexican vacation. A class act all the way!

Let's hear how Keenan became a Token Leader.

FROM THE PLAYING FIELD TO THE FINANCIAL FIELD

I was born and raised in Edmonton, but my dad is from Dominica, in the Caribbean. He moved here in his twenties and has the spirit of an entrepreneur. Growing up, I was part of a big, happy family. My dad ran an auto body shop, worked in construction, and did renovations. He may not have been wildly successful, but he had the perseverance of a true entrepreneur. Meanwhile, my grandpa was a farmer, managing his own business. Both were major influences on my own life as an entrepreneur, showing me that real success comes from hard work. As I grew up, I was really involved in sports in high school and university. I've always loved sports, but not just for the game itself—it's the camaraderie and teamwork that draw me in.

After university, I wasn't sure where to land. My dad's friend, a manager at Scotiabank, suggested I try being a teller over the summer. I quickly moved into personal banking after graduation, bouncing around, learning about mortgages—always with an entrepreneurial mindset. By 23, I'd bought my first house and, with a cousin, started building a property portfolio.

I wanted to know how to advance faster. At first, I got the advice to switch banks; I went to ATB Financial and did another five years there. It was a great place to work, but eventually the question came up again: *How do I grow? How do I go faster?* One of my managers told me, "If you want to climb the ladder, you'll either have to work here ten more years, or go get an MBA."

I chose the MBA route. Putting all my eggs in one basket, I applied only to UBC (The University of British Columbia) for their renowned Sauder program, drawn by the promise of international exposure and the solid network I'd already built. So, I went all in, attending UBC open houses and making connections there, determined to take this next step in my career. And I got in.

THE SEEDS OF TOKEN

After graduating from UBC, fate dealt me a strange hand. I was graduating just as the oil industry in Alberta took another hit. At ATB, I had an amazing internship focused on change management within the bank. But as the economy shifted, the department downsized and the woman I interned with was let go. They offered me a return to my previous role in sales and wealth management; I realized that wasn't for me. I decided to leave the organization.

A friend of mine, Cam, was working on a cannabis project that I'd been watching from the sidelines. It was a new, emerging market with no clear guidelines. Over a beer one night, Cam told me he had an idea for a line of cannabis beverages and needed someone to steer the project and help with raising capital. As a banker, I had some relevant experience. Cam had explored trying to bring a beverage to market, approaching various manufacturers in the then-Wild West of the cannabis space. But nobody knew how to structure that sort of manufacturing partnership, with everyone focused at the time on being either a grower or a retailer. I pointed out that there was a gap in the market—there was nobody in the middle doing manufacturing services for small cannabis businesses.

I said to Cam, "Why don't we just skip trying to find someone who can make our drink, and build out a facility that can make our own drinks?" That idea evolved into manufacturing for others as well, making Token into a cannabis manufacturing hub that could serve our own product needs and tap into the underserved need of others who wanted to put out their own small cannabis product lines. That's what kicked off my transition from banking to manufacturing.

I developed a business plan and began developing plans for a manufacturing facility, as Cam developed formulations. We were soon joined by our lead investor, Jamie, who quickly became much more than an investor and is still an integral member of the team and operations. When Token began, we were aiming to be a cannabis beverage brand. As it often goes with startups, we've evolved into a much larger operation.

THE WILD WEST

The early days of cannabis were crazy. The industry was being built while the plane was in flight, so there was no roadmap. I couldn't just find a business plan for a manufacturing facility, nor was there clear guidance on how regulatory bodies would handle applications or navigate the process. To add to the chaos, there was an influx of capital in the space. Due to this 'cannabis tax,' everything cost more than it should have because everyone assumed that with a cannabis license, you'd become a multimillionaire in no time, making it easy to raise money.

We were in a unique position where we didn't want to raise more than necessary. I think our modesty as young entrepreneurs saved us—we didn't want to grab $10 million right off the bat and start splurging, unlike many in the Canadian cannabis space who were just hoarding as much capital as they could. Everything was overpriced, and in the regulatory realm, even the government seemed clueless.

Often, when you'd ask the government for clarity, they'd just copy-paste the regulations you had already read and tell you to interpret them. This situation created both opportunities and pitfalls. Our interpretations could help shape the industry, but there was also a high chance of mistakes and wasting money trying to match their understanding of the rules. It was chaotic, but for those who remained focused and didn't overreach, there were a lot of opportunities. We managed to navigate this carefully and were able to slowly capture them.

START SMALL TO GO BIG

In the beginning, everyone was constructing massive facilities, thinking, "The big players have a hundred thousand square feet. I have ten thousand, so my valuation is a tenth of theirs." There was just so much capital flying around without due diligence. We almost fell into that trap, aiming to build a large facility. Our first model was $4 million—pretty small, in the cannabis space. We could have raised all the capital at once, but we'd just brought on a board of advisors. Some questioned why a young startup that hadn't made a dollar yet would invest in an advisory board. Free advisors are great, but when you pay, it's a different game—you gain access to people you otherwise couldn't reach. It was worth every dollar.

At our board meeting, I presented our blueprints—we'd already spent thousands on the design. We'd also invested about $140,000 in IP for an extraction system to kick off our company. But when one of our board members, Greg McGlone, who had experience with massive buildouts at Nutrium, saw the plans, he bluntly called it stupid. He asked, "Where's your pilot lab? Where's the proof of concept?" This was a total shift from the usual "build and figure it out later" mentality in cannabis at the time.

Instead of building our full facility at once, we constructed an even smaller $1.8 million space. This decision was critical. With a smaller footprint, we could pivot as needed and staff up gradually. As the industry fluctuated, we adapted. If we had taken all the capital and built like everyone else, basing our company's valuation on comparables, we probably would've been out of business years ago.

There were other surprising upsides of operating in a regulated market when you're a startup with limited funds. You become hyper adaptable. We lived to pivot. Being small levelled the playing field. Our voice counted just as much as the larger players. We could do grassroots events more efficiently than the bigger companies. People liked us because we were the little guys, and we had a large existing network we could tap into. Goliath doesn't win all the time.

TOKEN OFFERINGS

As we built the revised cannabis facility out, we were facing new challenges. We were a startup without the ability to generate revenue. The regulations were rapidly changing, which meant delays to the facility completion as we adapted to new stipulations. We knew it was going to be a long haul and we wanted to make money and we wanted to make things. So we got creative, and Token Bitters was born.

The extraction process for both cannabis and aromatic bitters is similar: you use ethanol to extract from plants. For bitters, you extract from fruits and spices; for cannabis, from the plant to get CBD and THC. Cam, who is a chemical engineer, suggested we start with bitters since they were simpler to produce. We were able to test extraction, flavour development, product creation, and supply chains in a test product. We could play with the brand,

and see what people responded to. We could get in front of our target market, legally. Bitters does not have the same restrictions as cannabis when it comes to advertising, social media, and sponsorships.

We began making bitters in my kitchen, but after a gnarly turmeric incident, my wife kicked us out to the garage. Our setup was simple: Everclear and a crockpot. We gave away our bitters to local bartenders for free, just asking for their feedback. Through some local network connections, bartenders started using our bitters in competitions and in menus, and we gained some recognition in Edmonton's cocktail scene.

Meanwhile, our investors saw we could produce a viable product. It wasn't a complex cannabis system, but bitters in 100-millilitre bottles that cost us $3 to make. That was our MVP. Soon, big chains like Liquor Depot started reaching out because customers were asking for Token Bitters, which they'd heard about from bartenders.

Since there was no existing framework for bitters, we approached Hanson Distillery and Strathcona Spirits Distillery to produce them. Within a year, we became Alberta's largest bitters company. This success caught the attention of the City of

Edmonton's export division, and the next year, we began selling our bitters internationally, starting with Japan. All this momentum helped us raise capital for our cannabis venture. Bitters weren't a huge moneymaker, but they provided a story we could get behind to build our brand and business.

TOKEN LEADERS

Diversity has always been a value around my leadership journey, and as I built my first real startup, diversity played a key factor in building the team of founders.

The three of us all came from unique backgrounds, and with that contrast, we were able to look at problems from three unique perspectives. We stood out in the community as Token team members.

Throughout the company's growth we've been really proud to represent a whole range of ethnicities, religions, languages, and nationalities. This has been great because all voices of our target audience are represented equally.

It was particularly valuable in the emerging markets such as cannabis—thanks to our unique perspectives, when everyone was looking right, we turned left.

NEW GROWTH IN CANNABIS

After years of waiting on regulatory approvals, we were granted our production license and, quickly after, a sales license to sell to the recreational market. Our focus on cannabis drinks quickly evolved. Irrational regulatory restrictions and taxation structures meant that drinks were prohibitively expensive and difficult to get consumer buy in for when the market opened. We followed the desires of the consumers and expanded first into gummies, chocolates, topicals and oils and later into vapes, flower, and pre-rolls.

We launched our own product lines and we worked closely with other small operators bringing their unique products to market. Regulatory bodies were a constant battle at every level, eating margins and restricting which brands had access to the recreational market.

The market still hasn't reached its potential, which isn't surprising as the first large country to legalize; there was no model to follow on what not to do. As the barriers popped up, we knew that while we believe in what cannabis offers, we wanted to expand into additional emerging product markets that support our overall goal of supporting small manufacturing and creating social alternatives to alcohol.

A NEW GENERATION, AN EMERGING MARKET

The next step for us has been the rapidly growing mocktail space, with bitters as the foundation. The story of how our bitters and mocktails evolved involves a woman named JoAnne who was creating a recipe book using our bitters for her mocktails. She approached us, knowing we had experience making bitters and bringing products to market. We suggested, "Give us your favourite mocktail recipe, and we'll bottle it for you." So, the bitters naturally transitioned into mocktails since they're a key ingredient.

Our Canadian distribution plan started aligning with this trend towards alcohol alternatives. COVID turned out to be a catalyst for this space. We essentially skipped two to three years' worth of new drinkers; 18-year-olds didn't get the chance to go to bars and have that defining social experience, leading to a gap of non-drinkers entering the market. And the high prices have also driven Gen Z away from drinking. Now, with a beer costing $9 and a cocktail $15, if there's no value in the social experience of drinking, why pay for an expensive hangover?

We saw the mocktail market getting busier, and we were at the forefront. As of now, we're on track to become Edmonton's top mocktail provider in the next few quarters. The plan is to expand across Canada, leveraging the inroads we've made with bitters. We're saying, "Here's a canned beverage following the trend, and by the way, it contains the bitters you already love." That's our plan for Canadian expansion.

Health Canada released a study about how many drinks a person should have in a month, and it suggested just two—a number far below what most people traditionally consume. I just got back from Mexico, and I'm pretty sure I exceeded that in just a few hours. There's this growing health consciousness. Alcohol might not become as taboo as smoking in our generation, but who knows how future generations will view it? Will it be considered really bad for you?

People are tracking their lifestyles with gadgets like the Oura Ring and WHOOP Bands, which highlight the impact of alcohol on sleep. It's becoming more visible, making people think twice about casual drinking on a weeknight. Now, the decision to drink alcohol seems more deliberate, reserved for social events where they're willing to compromise their health for the experience.

I don't think alcohol will ever disappear, but the casual drink at home might become less common. People are finding alternatives like cannabis or mocktails, and they're starting to reserve alcohol for social occasions.

FIVE-YEAR BUCKET LIST

For us, the big five-year plan is to become the leading manufacturing hub for social alternatives to alcohol in the country. If you're looking to bring a product to market, we're set up for collaboration and manufacturing. We already have a 60,000-square-foot yard and a 20,000-square-foot building up and running, and we're expanding. Our goal is to be the top manufacturer in this space—whether it's ready-to-drink cannabis, mocktails, or any new emerging market that arises, we want to lead the way.

ADVICE FOR YOUNG ENTREPRENEURS

I think the number one thing in entrepreneurship is a mix of steadiness and grit. You might think, "After this capital raise, we'll be set," or "Once we launch this product, it'll be smooth sailing." But that's a mindset that leads to burnout. There's no finish line where everything suddenly becomes easy.

You have to be ready for the goalposts to move. You reach one peak only to find there's another climb ahead. It's crucial not to get discouraged during these transformations. I always say to budding entrepreneurs, "It won't be a straight line." It's going to twist and turn, and it's about maintaining the mindset that there's no single end goal just a year away. The company will look different each year, and it'll keep improving.

You learn from your environment and get better at it. When I was at the bank, I didn't see myself becoming an entrepreneur. It's about exposure to opportunities and that spark of excitement that makes you think, "I can do this."

OPTIMISTIC REALISM

Entrepreneurs are optimists. They see a problem and think, "I can solve this, or I can find a team or help to solve it." Maybe we're a bit crazy, but there's this optimism that you can find a valuable solution to the problems you face.

But good entrepreneurs are also realists. Once you have an idea, it can be tough to let go of your "baby" that you might need to pivot away from, or to understand that as your team evolves, it changes. This was pivotal for us as our company grew. The staff who started the company aren't with us anymore. It's a completely different group now, except for a few. We evolved from two people to thirty, and even the first eight staff members have moved on. We're now on a different side of it. So, being realistic means understanding that we won't always be this happy, cute family that just rides off into the sunset together. It's more like, I need a certain skill set and team around me. And finding those pessimists is also important. I work closely with some of my team members who are absolute pessimists. They poke holes in all my ideas, but by the time they're done, I'm still positive that it will work. Now, I just have a strong case for how it will work because they've shown me things I completely missed.

THE IMPORTANCE OF BEING PRESENT

Early on, I had this intense focus on my business, and it often meant I was physically with friends or family or my wife, but my mind was always on my business. I had no sense of being present where I was. I don't know if I could've done it differently. Those first three to four years felt like there was no safety net; I just had to dive in fully. The real sacrifice was not being present and thinking about my business nonstop. As I've gotten older and more mature, I've learned the biggest lesson: to switch off. Now, I come home and understand there's no need to send emails at

11 pm. Nobody cares—you can wait until the next morning when work starts again. You don't have to be constantly on.

I try to meditate every morning, and I've had huge success in the past journaling. I spend the mornings unplugged; I walk my dog, and then sit on the floor for a five-minute meditation. I'm not extremely spiritual, but I believe in focusing inward to significantly improve your day. It's why even when things get hectic, I can stay calm. I try to start my day with tranquility.

It's important to find a way to reset when things get crazy. I ask myself, "What's my anchor?" For me, it's going for walks. I think, "Let's just go for a walk. Leave your phone." When I come back, I feel reset. It's all about finding that little thing you need to get back to your baseline.

SUCCESS AND SUCCESSION

My definition of success has started to change as I've gotten more into it. It used to be all about revenue and targets—that was success. But now, it's about building something scalable, something I can hand over and move around. I want to create a concept that others can take and improve upon, maybe even make it ten times better. That's the kind of legacy we'd leave in the market. So as we scale, I'm looking to see if this business can thrive without me. Can it keep running, and can we still hit our revenue and targets if I'm not at the building? It's about expanding to three different locations, with all of us running in the same direction. Success is watching these different parts work together.

As I've entered my fifth year as a CEO, I'm starting to think about succession planning and instilling it in our leadership group, removing roadblocks. I still love my job—every day feels like the best job I could have written for myself. But now, as the CEO and executive who gets all the attention and learning opportunities, I'm focusing on finding chances for our staff. For example, having our production supervisor lead a team in an incubator project, or exposing them to a networking event to push them out of their comfort zone. It's not just about staying within the four walls of our facility; it's about becoming community leaders, getting them on boards, and such. That's the succession plan I'm starting to implement—building a strong team around me and then figuring out what the next phase will be.

Although I started as the integrator at Token to Cam's visionary, I am now in the visionary role. While before I had to be the operator, I was soon able to hire others to take that role in their divisions. I don't grind over the details, and so I bring in team members who will. I have deep trust that my team and I will find solutions to any problem, and prefer to guide towards an end point rather than dictate the path to get there.

I was recently recognized in the Edify magazine's Top 40 Under 40 in the Edmonton scene. My business partner and my wife nominated me, and it was great to see others rally behind my story. I think what stood out was my involvement in the Edmonton community, which has a big city vibe but a small-town feel. Being active in networks, volunteering, and being present—those efforts came through with this award. Last year,

I received the Volunteer of the Year award at the YEG Startup Awards. I really believe that the more you give, the more opportunities come your way.

I always tell young entrepreneurs not to just sit behind a computer all day. Get out, contribute to the community, join a board, volunteer for causes that interest you. The connections you make are invaluable. Whenever I face a problem, I talk about it. I believe in manifestation, and I've found that by sharing your story or struggles, help comes out of the woodwork in surprising ways.

My personal journey is a timeline of learning and experiences, and both the highs and the lows set me up for success in the future. The journey you're on now is building your own foundation of experience. You're learning intensely from the highs and lows. Keep in mind that nothing is any one thing—every 'good' has a bad flip side and every 'bad' thing has good in it.

Keenan Pascal is the CEO and founder of Token Holdings, an Edmonton-based manufacturing company. Token Holdings is the parent company of Token Naturals, a cannabis manufacturing facility and a sister company Token Bitters which manufactures and distributes mocktails and cocktail accessories to local and international markets.

Prior to Token, Keenan spent more than eight years gaining financial and consulting experience at major banks paired with numerous entrepreneurial endeavours, angel investing, and an industrial and residential real estate portfolio.

Keenan has a Bachelor of Commerce from the University of Alberta and an MBA from UBC Sauder School of Business. With a mandate to stay engaged with his greater community, Keenan sits on the board of the Edmonton Downtown Business Association, Innovate Edmonton's Advisory Council and the University of Alberta's Business Advisory Council.

12

Beer for Life

Graham Sherman and Tool Shed Brewing Company

OST ENTREPRENEURS AND LEADERS ARE open and prepared for risk. Graham Sherman, a feisty and driven entrepreneur based in Calgary, Alberta, is someone who can handle risk. In fact, he thrives on the challenge.

Graham is a pioneer within the craft beer industry in Alberta who has had a major impact in getting government legislation changed so that small craft beer start-ups like his own had the ability to brew beer in the province.

In this chapter you will see what true courage and perseverance looks like: a fledgling entrepreneur whose back was against the wall from day one of starting his business. You will also discover what being vulnerable really looks like as a committed entrepreneur who wasn't too proud to cry into his "entrepreneurial pillow" when the going got tough.

I first met Graham when he spoke at an Edmonton business event in 2018 and was impressed by his entrepreneurial drive and commitment. While Graham and I stayed connected it wasn't until the spring of 2022 when we reconnected at an ACG (Association for Corporate Growth) Conference where I was serving as emcee. I was delighted to see Graham was one our keynote speaker for our opening reception. That sealed the deal for me. He was already on my list to participate in my new book, and this was the perfect opportunity to connect with him and share my vision for *Lunch with Leaders*.

While I tasted several of his different varieties of beer, my fave is "People Skills"; considering that my business, X5 Management, is in the business of helping people (Align Leaders and Teams to Achieve), the name of the beer really resonated with me, and so did the taste! I enjoyed my conversation with Graham. He is super outgoing and a dynamic guy who brings energy to every conversation!

A TOUGH BUT GREAT JOB

I worked in IT infrastructure before Tool Shed. It was a unique level of IT; we designed and implemented government and military SATCOM projects in war zones. You know the drill: NATO, secret clearance level, tactical type projects. For example, when a country goes in to help rebuild a place, like Afghanistan, the communication networks are really important. You need specially trained teams to design and install those networks. That's what the company I worked for did.

The thing is, those types of jobs are high level IT, operating in one of the worst environments on the planet. Coming into the job, many people feel appeased because they've obtained such a high-level position in their industry. They don't realize what a crazy career choice they've made and how the stress will keep them pumped up on adrenaline 24/7.

Even so, I loved my job. I always sought those projects out—probably because I'm a high-level geek. When I wasn't doing that, I sought hobbies that could appeal to my inner nerd. That's where the transition to home brewing began. To be honest, I never in a million years thought that my curiosity and inner nerd would make Tool Shed what it is today. But I guess it goes to show what happens when you take your hobbies way, way, *way* too far!

I was great at my job; to look at me, you'd have thought I would do that my entire life. But it was tough. I would be gone for six or seven months at a time with limited communication in a Third World country trying to put up communication networks. Some of the projects I was involved with I couldn't tell my family where I was going or what I was working on. There'd be extended periods of time where I was completely unable to communicate. That's a hard place to be when you have a wife and three kids. We couldn't see each other, or many times even talk to each other. It was tough. Exciting, but really tough!

FINDING YOUR PASSION

I have found that in life and business, there's a natural progression to things. It was the same with home brewing. First, I got into coffee beans, which amazed me because it appealed to my geekiness. I loved identifying all the variables of roasting coffee. It takes time; you can't just google it. You have to isolate all the variables, one at a time, and then try to control them so you can make better roasted coffee or espresso each time. Coffee was a huge obsession of mine, as was barbecue. (I'm like many entrepreneurs: shiny object syndrome!)

I love the world of barbecue because it's very similar to roasting coffee and brewing beer. If you're going to do an 18-hour slow and low smoked brisket, what are the variables that you're trying to control so that you can make a brisket good enough to make it to the World Championships of Barbecue? That's what appealed to my inner geekiness about brewing in the backyard tool shed. OH...and the fact that I really love beer! I'd travel to the States, visit these amazing breweries in California, Oregon, and Montana, and I'd hoard all this great beer and bring it home. For me, home brewing was the next logical step.

A RECIPE FOR CONNECTION

I think the biggest thing that really connected all those hobbies was my true passion. It has always been for service, hosting, and connecting with great people, sharing great times and stories. Beer is the catalyst that makes that happen more than anything else I've ever encountered in my life. Truly, this catalyst is what built Tool Shed. I started to see a community being built around it. Especially when everyone wanted to be at my place for the next Calgary Flames hockey game, the next poker night, or a UFC fight. It was the funniest thing. Literally, people were coming up with excuses for me to invite them over! They were figuring out reasons I could invite them to the backyard tool shed for good times with good people and good beers.

LET PASSION BE YOUR FUEL

The thing is, the more you do something with passion as your fuel, the more you want to do it. It doesn't exhaust you like it does when you're striving to compete in a job industry (that you hate) for 40 or 60 hours a week. I remember having a conversation with a buddy I was brewing with back then. I told him, "I think this is the freaking secret of life, man. You sleep like a baby at night when you make people happy all day."

Stop striving so you can start thriving.

Isn't it amazing how we, as human beings, can take something simple and make it so complicated? It's so tempting and easy to make our lives overly complicated by striving and striving to grow in our industry.

If you stop and take a moment to say, "What are we actually here to do?" It's exactly that: bringing great people together to share great times and great stories over great beer. That was the real catalyst for me taking that plunge and quitting my job.

NEXT LEVEL PASSION

That's the irony of being an entrepreneur. I'm definitely not someone who dips my toe in the water to test the temperature; I'm a light switch man. I'm either all on or all off.

To get into something like brewing beer, I really feel it took that high level of IT in a dangerous environment to give me the confidence that maybe I had what it took to start a business. If you can work in that insane an industry, and in that insanely dangerous environment, it's almost like a metaphor for being an entrepreneur.

When I think back on it now, I was probably trying to justify in my head that I had what it took to start a business. You go down this road of thinking, "But that's irresponsible, and I shouldn't be doing this. I should be just paying the bills. I'm middle-aged, I have three kids depending on me, and we have a mortgage." You have all this stuff that secures you in your well-paying government or military job, and then you think, "No, I have to set an example for my boys. I can't talk to them about going after things in life, taking risks, and following dreams if I'm not doing it." I had to talk myself into it.

I think I'm the World Heavyweight Champion at justifying in my mind what I want to do.

I believe we will always have an internal battle with following our dreams, especially if it seems irresponsible. No matter how many times I told myself, "It's for the kids. I have to do it for the boys," I still knew on the other side of that justification, I was our sole income at the time, and my wife hates beer! Believe me, it's not an easy conversation to have with your wife when you say, "Honey, what do you think about us quitting our well-paying job to make beer?"

Those conversations are never pleasant, which is proba-bly why people don't have them. Don't get me wrong; I'm not suggesting you start a business without discussing it with your spouse, nor am I suggesting you quit your job to start your own business. (I don't want anybody's spouses out looking for me!). I'm just saying that's how I did it. I'm an all-or-nothing, jump-in-with-both-feet kind of man.

FROM A GOVERNMENT JOB TO "ILLEGALLY" BREWING BEER

It's mind-blowing when you find yourself without a job doing something that's illegal in the province; that's a pretty big hur-dle to overcome! The legislation in our province was unreal, you couldn't start a brewery in Alberta, unless you could show the government you could brew 500,000 litres of beer a year or more. Perspective-wise, that would put you in the top 5% of breweries for size in North America.

- First, why on earth is that a law in the first place?
- How is that helping our province?
- Who contributes to this type of legislation where you hinder small business growth, especially agricultural economic development in Alberta?

Of course, the barrier of entry to most businesses, especially one as capital intensive as brewing, is cash. How do you raise millions of dollars? I don't have that kind of money, I used to make great money in Afghanistan. I just spent it all on stupid barbecues, and coffee roasters. Since I didn't have the money, I had to get the money from somewhere and let me tell you it wasn't easy.

THE BANKS LAUGHED

To start a brewery, there's an insane amount of capital required. And where do you naturally go for capital? To a bank, right? But what happens when the banks laugh at you? And investors laugh at you? Well, if you're like many entrepreneurs, you keep asking until they stop laughing.

Nobody likes asking for money; I get that. But you have to go to a bank if you want money for a business, right? The longest business relationship you'll have is with the person, the banker, who loaned you the money. Typically, you go in with a business plan and tell them what you want, and hopefully, they give it to you. But, of course, because I don't do anything the easy way, my presentation looked a bit like this: "I want to start a business. Here's what I want to do. Here's the plan." The bank laughed out loud, and the comment to me was, "A brewery? Well, that's adorable."

They used the word "adorable."

That was a humiliating experience, especially when you're putting everything into your dream. Just when I thought we were making progress in the province and getting people to know about our brewery, I go to the bank, and it's like, "Nope. Nope. Nope. Nope. Nope." It was unbelievable how many barriers we faced.

CRYING INTO YOUR ENTREPRENEURIAL PILLOW

Besides getting all the "nopes" left and right, let's go back to the 500,000 litres a year situation.

That's when the real entrepreneurial journey began. I had to think outside the box quickly because it seemed like we were encountering roadblocks at every turn.

And what really stood out to me was that nobody had done this before. There were really only two breweries at that time in the city of Calgary: Big Rock and Wild Rose.

I think there were 120 breweries in British Columbia at the time and 115 in Ontario. In Calgary, we had just a couple. I think 12 province wide. But what really blew my mind was that Lanny

McDonald (Former Professional Hockey player for the Calgary Flames) had a brewery, and it wasn't in Calgary. I thought, "Holy crap. Mr. Calgary has a brewery, and it's not here?" My mind would go to these negative places, thinking, "It probably won't happen. Because if Lanny McDonald couldn't do it, who am I?"

And that's a horrifying thought. I've gone all in, quit my job, and it might not even work. Many nights, I would have what I refer to as the three o'clock cry session. I'd get so stressed, staying up all night, which is typically when I do my best work. But I'd become so stressed out that I'd stay up crying into my entrepreneurial pillow.

OBSTACLES CREATE OPPORTUNITY

But it was during one of those sessions that we came up with the idea that if we couldn't brew beer in Alberta, maybe we should import beer. When you start to consider how beautiful the barley in this part of the world is, you realize Alberta barley is the best on earth.

The more I tried to persuade the Alberta Gaming and Liquor Commission to help change this legislation, the more I realized this was about something much bigger than just us and Tool Shed. It was really about putting Alberta barley farmers on the map.

So, what better way to do that than to say, "Okay, until we can get a brewery going, let's import beer, and we'll only import beers that use Alberta barley." That became my business plan. I went to the AGLC with this plan, and they said, "Yep, you can do that." So, we changed the whole business plan and became importers.

The moment we got that import agency license, we found a brewery just outside of Vancouver that would let us brew our beer in their facility. Essentially, this was my workaround. I'd export Alberta barley out of the province, brew with it across the border, and then come back to Calgary and import my own beer back into the province. It's totally insane!

AN ABSURD BUREAUCRACY

It's ridiculous how bureaucratic things can become. It makes absolutely no sense that I literally have to take Alberta barley out of the province to brew beer with it, and then import it back. Brewing beer with Alberta barley in Alberta isn't legal? Come on. It seems so insane. It sounds like it couldn't be true, right? But it was. That's how we started. As I speak to you right now, I'm in my truck, which has over 600,000 kilometres (Cad spelling) on this Tacoma. I've driven out to brew, driven back home, driven out again to package, and then back home, and so on. I've handled various challenges, and ultimately, I've delivered beer to people to share this story.

Be resourceful in raising capital if your bank merely finds you adorable.

By this point in the story, we had already successfully done our part to help change those laws. It was in December 2013 that the AGLC (Alberta Gaming and Liquor Commission) finally said, "Okay, no more minimum brewing requirement." They sent us a congratulatory tweet. It was a moment I'll cherish for the rest of my life. That acknowledgement from the AGLC was special. I know we weren't the only ones pushing for this change. But I believe our unique approach set us apart. Interestingly, there were people in litigation with the AGLC trying to force a change in this law.

I don't know if you've ever tried to sue the government to change a law, but it's not typically a strategy that helps your cause.

Our strategy was to rally a community of barley farmers to support our mission and back us up with studies that showcased the benefit to our province. It was this unconventional approach that made everything fall into place.

Operating a business without cash flow is like trying to live without oxygen.

In life, as in business, there are ups and downs, valleys and peaks. Just as we finished celebrating our victory in changing the law, we faced another massive challenge.

We were cash strapped. Multiple times along this journey, we found ourselves grappling with financial woes while trying to get the brewery off the ground. Most people don't comprehend the immense cost of starting a brewery. Millions and millions of dollars are involved.

Suddenly, you're placing deposits on stainless steel brewing equipment and securing a building, yet you can't even pay yourself. How were we to cover our home mortgage? Ultimately, I couldn't. At one point, I had three mortgages on my house, all facing foreclosure. Talk about stress!

UNDER PRESSURE

I believe that running a business is a fine art, balancing cash flow, inventory, and people, and knowing when to duck when things go south. As an entrepreneur, I believe it's critical to master the skill of remaining calm under pressure. I think I acquired that skill in Afghanistan, where situations were often a matter of life and death. Staying calm under such circumstances allowed me to think creatively and outside the box.

Ironically, though, I was never as afraid in Afghanistan as I have been while running a business. The difference isn't even close!

Speaking of fear, consider this situation. I recall when our home was in foreclosure. We couldn't cover the first month's rent on our building after putting down a $65,000 deposit on the lease. The rent was $15,000, and we didn't have it. My business partner approached me, saying, "We're in deep trouble. We need half a million dollars, or it's over for us."

"We can't cover the rent or any other expenses. Even if we meet all our targets, achieve all our sales goals, and construct the brewery on time and within budget, we'll still be half a million dollars short just in operating cash flow." Situations like this are where many businesses fold, and that realization terrified me.

If someone ever tells you that men shouldn't cry or don't cry, they're mistaken. I've shed many tears over the years, and I'm not ashamed to admit it. Let me take you back to one of those nights, when I was lamenting on my entrepreneurial journey at 3:00 AM. Amidst a particularly intense bout of crying, an idea struck me.

It's vital for entrepreneurs to think differently and to constantly exercise that innovative part of the brain which conjures disruptive, unique, and creative solutions.

That idea I had at 3:00 AM was what saved the brewery at that critical juncture. I thought, "What if we could get a hundred people to pay us $5,000 each, in exchange for Beer for Life?" The direness of our situation made even such a drastic solution seem appealing. At times, it felt like we were brawling in the streets, brainstorming any and every way to rescue our business. But then I thought, "If that's what it takes, then let's do it."

PARTNERS IN A CAUSE

After driving back and forth for brewing, packaging, and trying to establish the brewery, I would arrive completely exhausted in the evening. At that time, I would go to every bar, pub, and restaurant and talk to individuals one by one, pitching them on what I was doing.

"I'm starting this brewery. It's going to be amazing in two years. You'll receive Beer for Life, but I need five grand right now."

And that's how it was. I hit the streets with vigor. The first month was terrifying. I managed to get three people onboard, and that money allowed us to pay the rent, letting us continue for another month. It felt like an uphill battle.

Just as we began to feel a slight relief, the second month arrived, and our production facility failed to produce our beer. Consequently, we had no stock to sell. We had to compensate for both the production and cash flow shortfalls. We needed 40 grand that month. I thought, "I struggled to find three Beer for Life members last month; how will I find eight now?"

Yet, miraculously, two days before the month ended, I secured the eight members we needed, allowing us to push through for another month. Interestingly, one of our earliest supporters for the Beer for Life program was Big Rock Brewery.

Why would my competitor want a lifetime supply of my beer? They should be hoping for my failure rather than purchasing Beer for Life. Were they trying to steal my recipes? These thoughts raced through my mind.

But it turned out to be one of those remarkable moments in our journey. A predecessor in the industry set an example of collaborative thinking. It was so authentic of them to say, "We see you advocating not just for entrepreneurs, but also for barley farmers. We support your efforts in promoting agriculture in this province." They believed our voice needed to resonate more in Alberta.

"We can't champion this cause alone. We need more businesses sharing this narrative."

It was incredibly humbling to witness Big Rock's support. They purchased a Beer for Life membership from us but never actually claimed their beer. They visit regularly and, while they've always shown their support, they've never accepted free beer from us. It's amazing what can be achieved with a little help, even from competitors.

NAME INSPIRATION

We actually have four core beers: People Skills, Red Rage, Star Cheek, and Flat Cap Stout. These beers are available in what's called a toolbox. You can always purchase the mixer pack in this toolbox.

Every summer, we release seasonal beers. Our Passion Fruit Blonde Ale will be out this summer because it's truly spectacular.

How did the name "People Skills" come about, and what's its backstory?

The man depicted on the can of People Skills is named Joe Greenwood. He is, without a doubt, the most difficult person I've ever encountered—there's no close second. I don't say that

in a playful way, like when you jokingly tell a friend, "Hey, man. I love you, but you're acting like a jerk." Joe is genuinely challenging to work with, to the point that I nicknamed him "People Skills" due to his complete lack of them.

When he would call, my ringtone for him was a line from the movie "Office Space" where a character exclaims, "What the hell is wrong with you people? I have people skills!" Naturally, he wasn't fond of that ringtone.

He was ex-military from New Jersey and worked on Afghan National Army and National Police contracts out there. Good old

People Skills was a project manager, and it was unbelievable the things he would do to upset everyone around him.

I found it hilarious to consider putting the biggest jerk I know on a beer can because I believe everyone knows someone like that in their life. I love the idea that you could buy a six-pack and say, "I'm going to leave this on your desk, Mike. Work on this; it's my treat." We all have that person in mind whom we'd love to buy a six-pack of People Skills for and simply tell them, "Work on this."

The funny part is Joe was quite upset about us depicting him on the can. While it's a cartoon, it's also a spitting image of him. His name is Joe Greenwood, so we used green wood on the can to ensure he recognized it was him. The most amusing thing is his mother found the whole situation hilarious.

BEER FOR LIFE

That's a great title because it also depicts my life. It's "Beer for Life" now. I've put my stake in the ground, and the "Beer for Life" membership saved us. I think it's great on multiple levels.

What we've learned along this journey is that we think we have businesses that have products that people will care about. Really, no one cares about your products but you. This is a never-ending question: how do we market and create an experience that people genuinely care about?

ALBERTA BARLEY SUPREMACY

How do we get people to care? In my experience, people care when you're doing great things for others. When it's about something authentic and genuine, and you can see the passion in the journey, that's what people get behind. People want to support a passionate story. When you can find a way to market your business that isn't just about you and your products, but truly about building it up—like uplifting Alberta barley farmers—so the world knows, that's impactful.

I'm not saying that Saskatchewan barley is any less valuable; Western Canadian barley is probably the best way to describe it. It's something we have, which is the best on earth, yet we don't really take credit for it. I get excited when I see how Napa Valley has claimed the excellence of their wine. That's where the best grapes grow. There's no difference here. The whole world should know: when you want the best beer, you go to where the best barley grows. That marketing story begins to tell itself. Your journey should be about elevating those barley farmers.

My passion in this industry has been getting to know these remarkable families. Many of them are fifth or sixth generation farmers. One that I always love to mention is Antler Valley Farm. Located just outside of Innisfail, Alberta, they are a fifth-generation farm. Young men who recently purchased the farm from their father. Naturally, the father still lives and works on the farm, but he's passed the torch to his sons. They had to secure millions of dollars from the bank to clear loans and buy out their father. It's like a genuine purchase. The succession of a farm is significant. Observing the equipment these young men operate to produce the best barley in the world is truly awe-inspiring. We believe their story is a compelling one for us to share.

When you share a story that's bigger than yourself, people are drawn to that passion for a genuine, authentic cause.

We don't use billboards. We display our logo on combines. These combines traverse the barley fields along Highway 2, between Calgary and Edmonton. As you drive that route, you might be unaware of the activities on the roadside, stretching all the way to Edmonton. But when you spot a massive Tool Shed combine, you realize, "Holy crap! They're cultivating beer in these fields!"

That recognition was a tremendous honor for us. An outstanding company from Nürburg, Germany, reached out, expressing, "My goodness, this is so cool. What's the story behind this combine and these farmers?" Our response was simple: "That's our connection." We want to emphasize the symbiotic relationship between the farm and the brewery.

DON'T DRINK BAD BEER

To give you an example of why I used to attend these Barley Growers meetings and the Barley Association meetings: I'd meet these guys, and when I walked into the room, they'd be drinking poor-quality, macro beer. I'd get up on stage and start giving them a hard time. I'd say, "You're not even drinking real beer. That's made with rice; it's subpar. You're not drinking actual beer." The example I gave was this: if you farmers send your kids off to university and don't care about their chosen careers, it's analogous to this situation. You're sending the best barley on earth out into the world and are unaware that it's used in the finest beers.

You need to start realizing that. You should be drinking those superior beers. The response I received from a farmer was spot on. He asked, "Alright, what kind of barley should I be growing?" I was taken aback and replied, "Two-row?" He responded, "Yes, obviously two-row. But which variety? Harrington, Metcalf, Copeland, or Synergy?" I admitted, "I have no idea. I'm unfamiliar with the specifics." So, there we were, both aiming for excellence in the same province for the same reasons, yet unaware of each other's expertise. Isn't that often the case?

It was a turning point for us, realizing, "Wow, we should collaborate more closely, testing different barley varieties. What would the differences in taste be?" There's so much potential for collaboration. This collaboration was what intrigued the company in Nürburg, Germany. They visited us, then invited us to the World Beer Show, putting us on stage to explain to German brewers the significance of this relationship. Consider this: these German breweries have been in operation for longer than our country has existed. And here we were, just a few years into our journey, sharing our insights on such a prominent platform, along with these dedicated farmers. Our story underscores the deep bond between the brewery and the farm.

ADVICE TO THE YOUNG

There's such a fear out there of failure. I get it; we all have it. I think it's innate in us; we don't want to be embarrassed. We don't want to fail. That fear of failure can cripple us, handcuff us, and prevent us from achieving greatness.

"Our deepest fear is not that we are inadequate.
Our deepest fear is that we are powerful beyond measure."
—Marianne Williamson

That is a beautiful quote. Our greatest fear is that we're powerful beyond measure and capable of incredible things. I've learned to embrace fear. As I mentioned, I was never as fearful in Afghanistan as I was when starting a business.

Because all of the challenges I've faced were beyond my expertise, outside of my comfort zone. Who am I to think that I can tackle the next challenge, raise millions of dollars, or undergo a national expansion?

I believe that finding comfort in fear is one of the most valuable lessons for people. When you feel fear, that's when you know you're in the right place, pushing your boundaries. Fear is beneficial. In fact, John Mayer has a great line in one of his songs: "Fear is a friend who's misunderstood."

GRAHAM'S BUCKET LIST

I don't know if we've discussed this before; maybe we have or haven't. But I know I've mentioned to you that I do ultra-marathons. I participate in Iron Man triathlons and ultra-marathons, but I don't really train. Sometimes, I sense when I'm becoming stagnant, and I know I have to push my boundaries. I need to get in over my head again. Sometimes, you head out into the mountains and run for 200 kilometers, and you shouldn't be able to do it. I haven't done the training to pull it off! A doctor would say it's impossible for me to do, but you just keep running, right? You just keep pushing up that mountain. It hurts like hell. You lose all your toenails, but it's such an incredible metaphor for what I have to go through next in my business. You always have to keep running forward, right?

One of my most influential mentors in running, when I embarked on this huge 200 km run in Colorado, simply said, "Graham, every time it hurts so much that you think you can't do it, just keep 'relentless forward progress' in your mind. Always, relentless forward progress, keep moving forward, right?" It's so good, right? So, whatever comes next, you never freaking know. No one in a million years could have predicted COVID, except for Bill Gates, I guess, who foresaw the pandemic. But when these kinds of things happen, they present opportunities to say, "Okay, I'm scared. I might go out of business because 70% of my customers are bars, pubs, and restaurants, all of which suffered during the pandemic." You go home and cry into your pillow in the middle of the night, but then you figure out what to do. You just have to keep tapping into that creative, disruptive part of your mind that sometimes only fear can access. When your back is firmly against the wall, you can come up with some really innovative solutions once you embrace that fear.

So, I thought, coming out of the pandemic, I sensed that dreadful little inkling of complacency creeping in. "Now we're good. We made it through the pandemic.

Am I getting too comfortable?" Because that's dangerous to me. So, I have to go out and take a big run in the mountains to push myself back into a fearful place. That's when we started working on the national rollout for our products.

FINAL ADVICE

I would say that the most important thing is, I don't know if everybody thinks the same way I do, but I never set out to do this thing, thinking that I was a leader or going to be one. I set out to do something that I thought was a good cause. And it was supporting great things in our province, in our community and our economy. And I looked up to the people who I looked at as leaders, and I looked at them like they were from Mars, because they just had accomplished such great things. And I just think "Who are these guys?" They have different blood or something. And I'll never be that guy. That guy is so far up on this ladder, and I think we all do that.

We hold people up on pedestals, thinking that they're these great leaders that have gone before us, and we're not them.

Once I caught myself in this pointless way of thinking I just focused on putting my head down and going after it. Every time I got into one of these fearful moments, I reached out to the people around me who are on similar entrepreneurial journeys.

You need those other leaders in your community. And the reassuring surprise is that they're all struggling with the same things, whether they admit it or not, some of their homes are in foreclosure, some are struggling to make payroll and they probably don't look at themselves as leaders either! Everybody's going through this stuff and when the moment you can be vulnerable and open and honest with the people around you and share these things, well, holy crap—what comes back is tenfold.

Creating a strong team of leaders around you is essential. As you share your challenges and learn from theirs, you'll sharpen your skills. Before you know it, you'll be looking down from the top of the ladder, with others wondering how you made it all happen. It's amazing to witness the entrepreneurial journey come full circle like that.

Graham Sherman is a self-professed "high level geek" who used his love of technology to disrupt an entire industry. In 2013, Sherman took homebrewing "too far" when he launched the Tool Shed Brewing Company. What was originally a hobby in his backyard tool shed is now a 22,000 square foot brewery with product sold in over 1000 locations. Sherman has been nominated for Canadian Entrepreneur of the Year, was named one of Calgary's 2016 "Top 40 Under 40" by Avenue magazine and won the 2018 Business in Calgary Leaders Award.

Conclusion

This book has been a true labour of love for me, ever since I came up with the concept back in the fall of 2021.

As I conclude *Lunch with Leaders*, it is my wish that each of you that took the time to read this book has taken away valuable lessons that you can apply to your business and personal life.

In business and in life, there are many pivotal moments that shape us and our direction—and there will be many more of those moments in the years to come.

I am reminded of the many takeaways from one of my favourite books from the past few years: *The Gap and the Gain: The High Achievers' Guide to Happiness, Confidence, and Success*, created by Dan Sullivan, Founder of Strategic Coach, along with Dr. Benjamin Hardy. The book states that "most people, especially highly ambitious people, are unhappy because of how they measure their progress. We all have an "ideal," a moving target that is always out of reach. When we measure ourselves against that ideal, we're in "the *Gap*." However, when we measure ourselves against our previous selves, we're in "the *Gain*."

The leaders that I had the privilege of interviewing in *Lunch with Leaders* had to pivot many times and couldn't always predict that the pivot—or their decision—was the right move at the time. Only time could allow them to look back and learn from the situation and the decision made. Sometimes we get it right, and all is well. But sometimes we don't get it quite right and need to learn from the past—which is the *gain*, whether it was success, or failure. This is growth, wisdom, and hindsight that allows us as leaders to make another decision when called upon.

I look at my own entrepreneur journey since 2006 and see that I, too, had to pivot on many occasions. The 'gains' made during those times were invaluable to me and my own leadership growth, even though not all gains were winners, and often my greatest lessons learned were in times of failure or significant challenge.

If you are a leader or entrepreneur who has just finished reading this book, I truly hope that you can reflect on your own pivotal moments of your past business journey. May you discover more 'gains' as you had to pivot through business and life. I'm certain you'll find far more than you realized.

If you enjoyed this book, I would love to hear from you and would welcome any comments via email: *mike@x5management.com*. Additionally, a review on Amazon.ca would be a kind gesture; I'd appreciate that greatly!

If you see value in this book for aspiring leaders or seasoned entrepreneurs, I would be most grateful if you share the book with them as a suggested read.

Best wishes to each of you in your personal and business journeys and may you pivot in the right direction when you are faced with challenging times or unique opportunities.

Sincerely,
Mike

Acknowledgments

There are so many people to thank along the journey of completing my book over the past 2+ years.

I'd like to begin with my late father-in-law, Hugo Lehmann, who was like a father to me since we met in 2011.

I had the good fortune to play chess with him on many occasions, where he won 95% of the time. Something he shared with me during one of our chess matches has stuck with me to this day. He said: "*Mike, you always play to not lose, but you never play to win*" which meant I played a defensive game versus an offensive strategy to win the game. How true is this in business and in life. I now aspire to win, more than lose.

He moved to Canada from Germany in 1954 with hopes for a better future. While it was an exciting time for Hugo, he was terribly sad to leave Germany and his family behind. But even though it was difficult, Hugo realized that he had nothing to lose and hopefully everything to gain. It was a pivotal moment in his life, a decision that ultimately shaped his future.

In May 1969 Hugo was able to open his own business called Freeway Auto Body with a new modern facility. He had four employees at the time. But just one month into his new business, he went through a major challenge when a huge explosion engulfed his back shop with two young men trapped inside who lost their lives that day. As he has stated many times, it was the worst experience in his life; incredibly tragic.

In his lifetime, Hugo experienced many emotional highs and lows. In his words: I could have easily remained in an emotional state; however, reality made me wake up and face the real world.

A sincere thank you to each leader who took the time to share their story and business journey for my book. I am grateful for each of you: Angela, Bruce, Chuck, Graham, Henri, Keenan, Koleya, Mary, Richard, Ron, Shannon, and Shawn.

Much gratitude and thanks to Curtis Stange for his generous contribution to write the foreword of my book. My respect and admiration for you as a leader, and long-time friend since 1986, is one that I value and treasure a great deal. A huge congratulations to Curtis on winning a 2023 Canada's Most Admired CEO Award in the Enterprise category!

To my beautiful wife Bonita Lehmann, who continues to be at my side every step of the way and supports me in my entrepreneurial and life journey. There are countless things that would not be possible in my world without you. I love you with all my heart!

Thank you to Miles Rote, who was one of the first book publishing experts that I talked to, in early 2022. Your guidance and recommendations were key to getting this book completed, even during the dark days of significant publisher adversity.

Thank you to Meghan McCracken, Founder & CEO of Brilliant Media and Windermere Press for the hands-on support over the past eight months of the book journey after I had to make a major pivot due to the demise of my first publishing firm. From editing to publishing and marketing, you were a delight to work with, and I trusted everything that you suggested, and it is reflected in the finished product.

To all of my valued business connections who took the time to contribute to a blurb or comment about the book, I thank you!

Finally, I am most grateful to everyone who took the time to buy and read my book and recommend it to others. Thank you.

About the Author

Mike Mack is the President of X5 Management, and is a sought-after Executive Coach, Consultant, Trainer, and Facilitator. He has been helping businesses maximize their potential since 2006. He is a two-time Amazon bestselling author of *Remarkable Service: How to Keep Your Doors Open* and *Relationships for Keeps: How to Build Powerful Relationships in Business and in Life.*

Mike holds an MBA from Athabasca University and is a proud member of Synergy Network (Edmonton, Alberta Canada), serving as Chair in 2016; Member of ACG (Association for Corporate Growth), serving as President in 2019 for ACG Edmonton; Past member of Toastmasters International, obtaining his Distinguished Toastmasters Designation—DTM. Mike lives in Edmonton, Alberta.

For more information on Mike and X5 Management, visit: *www.x5management.com.*

Connect with Mike on LinkedIn.

Recommended Reading

The Bold Ones: Innovate and Disrupt to Become Truly Indispensable,
Shawn Kanungo

Think Do Say: How to Seize Attention and Build Trust in a Busy,
Busy World, Ron Tite and Tite Tank Inc.

The 5 Levels of Leadership: Proven Steps to Maximize Your Potential,
John C. Maxwell

The Gap and the Gain: The High Achievers' Guide to Happiness,
Confidence, and Success, Dan Sullivan and Dr. Benjamin Hardy

Never Eat Alone: And Other Secrets to Success, One Relationship at
a Time, Keith Ferrazzi and Tahl Raz

The One Thing: The Surprisingly Simple Truth About Extraordinary
Results, Gary Keller and Jay Papasan

www.ingramcontent.com/pod-product-compliance
Lightning Source LLC
Chambersburg PA
CBHW050526190326
41458CB00045B/6726/J